Exploring the Kaw Valley

A guide to the natural and historic treasures
of the Kansas River Valley

By Lynn Byczynski

Exploring the Kaw Valley: A guide to the natural and historic treasures of the Kansas River Valley

Copyright photos printed by permission:
Steve Mulligan, front cover, back cover (2), 144, 148.
Joyce Wolfe, pages 16, 18, 26, 36, 38, 40, 42, 52, 54, 67, 68, 71, 72, 77, 79, 86, 97, 103, 104, 105, 108, 109, 116, 118, 120, 126, 128, 130, 133, 135, 139, 140.
Craig Thompson, pages 30, 46.
Janet Majure, page 59, 88.   Marty Birrell, page 95.   Michael Watkins, page 94.

Map credits
Kansas Department of Transportation, page 11.
Jackson Morley, pages 21, 34, 49, 62, 100, 110, 125, 142 (source: Kansas Department of Transportation).
Fred Holthaus (Kansas Department of Transportation), page 82.

Funding in support of this publication has been provided by an Environmental Protection Agency Community-Based Environmental Protection program grant; a National Park Service Rivers, Trails, Conservation Assistance program grant; Western Resources; Ronald J. and Joyce A. Wolf; Latane Donelin; and the Anna J. Brecount Trust.

Published by Breadbasket Publishing Company, P.O. Box 1161, Lawrence, Kansas, 66044, in association with the Kaw Valley Heritage Alliance, 414 E. 9th Street, Suite B, Lawrence, Kansas, 66044, www.kvha.org.

Library of Congress Control Number: 2002105496
ISBN: 0-9656695-7-2

Manufactured in the United States of America

To Joyce Wolf, founding director of the Kaw Valley Heritage Alliance, who has worked tirelessly to celebrate and preserve the natural beauty of Kansas.

About the Author

Lynn Byczynski first visited the Kansas River Valley in 1977. She was so impressed that she flew home to Pennsylvania, packed her bags, and moved to Kansas immediately. She is a flower farmer in rural Lawrence and the publisher of Growing for Market, a national monthly newsletter about direct-market farming. She is also the author of *The Flower Farmer: An Organic Grower's Guide to Raising and Selling Cut Flowers* (1997, Chelsea Green Publishing). She can be contacted at growing4market@earthlink.net.

Acknowledgements

This book would not have been possible without the inspiration, advice, and hard work of all the volunteer members of the Kaw Valley Heritage Alliance. They envisioned the project and worked for many years to bring it to life. Every one of them deserves credit.

I would also like to thank several people who made the writing of this book easier:

✔ Donn Teske of Wheaton showed me the back roads of Pottawatomie County and shared his extensive knowledge of the history of the area.

✔ Joy Lominska of rural Lawrence guided me to important sites in Jefferson County.

✔ Michael Watkins of the U.S. Army Corps of Engineers advised me on the bald eagle nest at Clinton Lake and provided photographs.

✔ Several other scientists provided guidance on technical and scientific matters: Teresa Rasmussen and Andy Ziegler of the U.S. Geological Survey; Paul Liechti and Kelly Kindscher of the Kansas Biological Survey; and Bob Angelo of the Kansas Department of Health and Environment.

✔ Dan, Will, and Laurel Nagengast accompanied me on many of the driving tours and shared my enthusiasm for the sites we visited.

✔ Steve Mulligan of Moab, Utah, generously donated the use of the gorgeous photographs on the cover.

✔ Janet Majure did a meticulous job of editing the manuscript, selecting photographs to illustrate it, and molding everything into a beautiful and readable book.

✔ Jackson Morley edited the photographs and adapted maps provided by the Kansas Department of Transportation.

✔ Fred Holthaus of KDOT created a sample map and assisted in the use of maps from the department.

Contents

Introduction

If you've ever had the pleasure of driving around a new place with a native who knows it well and loves it, you already know the kind of guidebook we have attempted to present here. We want you to be able to take this book on day trips and feel as though you have a tour guide sitting beside you, pointing out sites where events big and small have occurred, regaling you with stories, and explaining the unfamiliar features of the landscape. We hope that you will deepen your understanding of the land and its inhabitants. Mostly, we hope that you will learn to see the Kansas River Valley with new eyes, to appreciate its beauty and heritage, and to cherish this place we call home.

We refer to the Kansas River Valley, or Kaw Valley, in the title and throughout this book, but we realize that many people think of the Kaw Valley as the little strip of bottomland along the river. We might be more correct to refer to the Kansas River Watershed, but we were afraid the word "watershed" in the title might dilute our audience, if you'll pardon the pun.

A watershed is an area of land drained by a river and its tributaries. It is a scientific concept rather than a way we normally define "place." Instead, we tend to identify with political divisions - our city, our county, our state. But those divisions are more or less arbitrary, determined long ago by political issues. Kansas is a big rectangle whose borders were drawn by Congress. Only the little squiggle in the northeast corner—the Missouri River—reflects any natural features. The same is true with most counties. They are, essentially, just lines on a map.

A watershed is a natural way to divide up places. We are tied together by the rivers that run through our land. Our drinking water, the source of all life, comes from our watershed. Our businesses and industries, sources of livelihoods, depend on water. Heavy rain in the upper reaches of the river may cause flooding far downstream. Drought in the west can cause water rationing in the east. Pollution upstream can ruin a family picnic downstream. Rural or urban, we all belong to the same community of water.

The Kansas River watershed, which includes the river itself plus all its tributaries, is a huge drainage area—60,000 square miles of land in Kansas and Nebraska. The Kansas River itself is 170 miles long, beginning at the confluence of the Smoky Hill and Republican Rivers in Junction City, and ending where the Kansas River pours into the Missouri River in Kansas City, Kansas. The counties on both sides of the river are what we call the Kaw Valley. More than half the state's population lives in those 10 counties, making the Kaw Valley a very important region.

We created this tour guide as part of our work for the Kaw Valley Heritage Alliance, a non-profit organization dedicated to promoting greater awareness, appreciation, and stewardship of the cultural and natural resources of the Kaw Valley. The KVHA is made up of many partner groups interested in the quality of life in this region. Partners include schools and colleges, government agencies, businesses, economic development groups, and agricultural, arts, civic, conservation, cultural, historical, and recreational organizations. All these groups understand that our quality of life depends on taking a holistic approach to our region, on recognizing that all parts of our society must work together and in balance to make the most of the many resources we have here in eastern Kansas.

Committees of the KVHA worked for months to identify all the important historical, recreational, ecological, and cultural sites in the Kaw Valley. They also created a list of concepts that they wanted to include in the book—features that apply to the land in general rather than one site in particular. We compiled all those sites and concepts, plotted them on a map, and broke them into segments that can be visited in a half-day or so.

Aldo Leopold wrote this remark in *A Sand County Almanac*: "We abuse land because we regard it as a commodity belonging to us. When we see land as a community to which we belong, we may begin to use it with love and respect."

The Kaw Valley is our community. And it is a land of great natural beauty, awesome biological diversity, and fascinating human history. We hope that this guidebook will help you get out there and enjoy it.

Lynn Byczynski, author
Teresa Rasmussen, president, Kaw Valley Heritage Alliance
March 2002

How to use this book

The tours in this book are designed to introduce you to important cultural, historical, and natural resources in the Kansas River Valley. The tours begin at the east, along the Missouri River, and move west toward Junction City, where the Kaw begins. You will be following the river, weaving north and south about 30 miles in each direction through the watershed.

The trips range from those where you will mostly drive through the countryside to tours where you will spend most of your time on foot. Each tour is designed to take about four hours, not including travel time to the tour's starting point. You may spend more or less time on each trip, depending on whether you linger or breeze through.

The chapters cover one tour apiece, and, at the beginning of each chapter, you will find a map of the complete itinerary. Although each tour was created with some attempt at a cohesive progression, no harm is done if you scramble the order in which you visit the sites. Nor is it necessary to start your Kaw explorations with Tour 1 and work your way west.

Each trip stands on its own in explaining the history and ecology of the places you will visit, but they are not repetitive, even when the landscape or history seems to be. Concepts or events that are significant in several places are explored in detail only once. A reference to that section appears when those ideas are mentioned elsewhere. For example, the importance of fire in prairie ecosystems is relevant everywhere in eastern Kansas, which was once covered with tallgrass prairie. Prairie fires are explained in detail in Tour 10, on a visit to the Konza Prairie. In other tours where fire is significant, you will find a brief mention of it with a reference to the explanation in the Konza Prairie tour.

Throughout the book, you will find a special logo to designate places of particular interest to young children. These are mostly open spaces where kids can expend some energy without disturbing others. A few such indicators point out activities specially geared to children. That doesn't mean kids won't enjoy the rest of the tours; there are plenty of delights for children everyplace you will go.

On every trip, you will find places suitable for a picnic, if you want to bring your own food along. Otherwise, you will find places in towns on every tour where you can eat and find rest rooms.

The sites identified on these tours are by no means all there is to see and do in the Kaw River Valley. Many places were omitted because a half-day trip simply doesn't allow you to see everything. Others were omitted because they are such big attractions already—the Museum of Natural History at the University of Kansas, or the Capitol in Topeka—that you probably have already seen them.

The sites you will visit were chosen because they provide visual representations of specific facets of life in the Kaw Valley. When you stand in the places where history happened, and when you touch, smell, and feel the natural world, you will discover or deepen that "sense of place" that every resident should have about his or her home.

Leavenworth

The first tour takes place in the city of Leavenworth, where you can easily spend a full day exploring the area's history. Children will love this tour. It includes plenty of open spaces good for stretching little legs and burning off energy, and the Fort Leavenworth museum brims with fascinations for children and adults alike. Limited driving is required once you reach Leavenworth, and no special clothes are required, unless you'd like to climb down a bluff to the Missouri River.

Leavenworth is on a small strip of land in the northeast corner of Kansas that is in the Missouri River watershed. Since this is a book about the Kansas River watershed, you may wonder why we have included this city. We do so primarily to give you some context for the Kaw Valley tours ahead.

Leavenworth was the gateway to the Kansas River Valley for white settlers, and much of what happened in Leavenworth in the 19th century ties in to events in the Kaw watershed thereafter. Second, the city has some excellent historical resources that pertain to the settlement of the Kaw Valley. Finally, the Missouri River is a much different river from the Kaw, and visiting it first will deepen your understanding of the Kansas River when you explore it later.

Fort Leavenworth Military Reservation

Start at Fort Leavenworth, which is on the north side of town, on U.S. 73. After you pass through the gate, stop at the small visitor's building on your right and pick up a tour brochure. As you drive up the broad, tree-lined avenue, you will notice that Fort Leavenworth looks more like a college campus than a military installation. On weekends, you might not see anyone in uniform.

In fact, education is the main focus at Fort Leavenworth. The U.S. Army Command and General Staff College here is the Army's senior tactical school, a 10-month program in which officers from

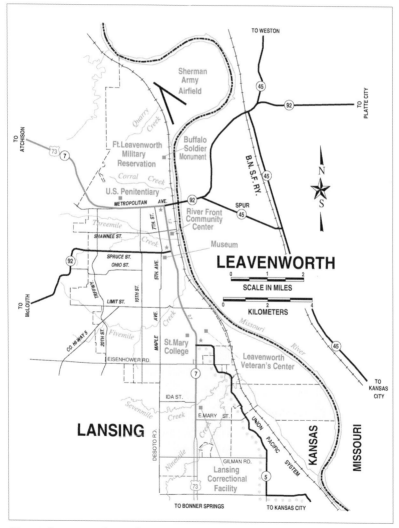

Tour 1: Leavenworth, a collection of sites rather than a tour route.

all services and from other countries train to lead fighting units. The college also houses the National Simulation Center, a sort of computer war game program. Fort Leavenworth has more officers than enlisted men and women, and no active units are stationed here except Military Police. Fort Leavenworth is considered more of a "think tank" than a base and consequently is one of the Army's most elite institutions.

The Missouri River

Following the map on the back of the brochure, first head for

Taming the Missouri

In the years before settlement, the Missouri changed course dramatically, relocating 2,000 feet or more per year in some places and depositing huge amounts of silt in other places. The constant erosion of the banks caused the river to carry a heavy load of silt and earned it the nickname "Big Muddy." Erosion and deposition created one of the most diverse ecosystems in North America, as the constantly shifting river created braided channels, chutes, sloughs, islands, sandbars, and backwater areas.

Native wildlife evolved along with the rise, fall, and meandering of the Missouri, and came to depend on it for seasonal habitats and reproduction. Each year, as snow melted in the Rocky Mountain headwaters of the Missouri and storms dropped rain on the Great Plains, the Missouri River flooded, creating wetlands that served as habitat for fish and the creatures that feed on them. The rising river and rising water temperatures provided the cues for fish to spawn. Spring torrents scoured away brush that had overgrown sandbars the previous summer.

But the wild ways of the Missouri River were an obstacle to white settlers, who wanted to farm its fertile floodplain, use its water for industries and towns, and navigate it for trading. Legislation passed in 1912, and reaffirmed many

the river to get the lay of the land. You can get a good view from the French Cannons area. From the bluff, you can see the power of the Missouri River and the landscape that surrounds it—the flat bottomland on the Missouri side and the tall bluffs on the Kansas side. For those who want to get out and hike, a rough stone stairway and an even rougher steep path lead to the access road beside the railroad tracks below.

The fertile bottomland across the river is owned by the Army and for many years was farmed by inmates at the U.S. Disciplinary

times thereafter, showed the nation's determination to tame the Missouri for navigation, development, and flood control. Engineering work begun in 1944 and officially completed in 1981 transformed the free-flowing river into a highly controlled channel.

Today, 35% of the river is impounded by dams to regulate the flow year-round and reduce flooding, and 32% is channelized to maintain a single, deep channel shaped into smooth, easy bends for navigation. Jetties like the one directly across the river from Leavenworth stabilize the bank and allow the adjacent land to be farmed.

The tradeoff for flood control has been the loss of a half-million acres of wildlife habitat in the 735 miles from Sioux City, Iowa, to St. Louis. Channelization shortened the river 72 miles; water habitat was lost as sediment collected behind wing dikes, creating new land; levees cut off wetlands from the spring flooding that recharged them; and 354,000 acres of floodplain where the river had once meandered were lost to urban development and farming.

The Corps of Engineers acknowledged the damage to fish and wildlife habitat when it began the Missouri River Fish and Wildlife Mitigation Project in 1986. The goal is to acquire and restore 28,000 acres along the river, about 5% of the habitat lost because of the stabilization projects.

Barracks at Fort Leavenworth. Now the bottomland is leased to local farmers. That farmland and the bluff where you're standing most likely would not be here today if the Missouri River had been left in its natural state.

In 1827, the War Department sent Col. Henry Leavenworth to establish a fort on the east side of the river. Leavenworth realized that the west side would be a better place for protecting the trails that were just beginning to be used for trade and settlement. His choice proved a good one: Leavenworth is the oldest continually operating Army fort west of the Mississippi.

Lewis and Clark expedition

On June 30, 1804, the Lewis and Clark expedition sailed, rowed, and poled their boats up the river here. Meriwether Lewis, the biologist of the expedition, spent much time ashore studying the animals and plants that were then strange to the people of the United States. He collected specimens and noted physical characteristics of the land such as the presence of springs, soil fertility, and likely sites for trading posts and homesteads.

Unfortunately, none of his notes for the spring and summer of 1804 have been found. All we have are the comments of William Clark, who spent most of his time on the keelboat.

"Deer to be seen in every direction and their tracks are as plenty as Hogs about a farm," he wrote on June 30, after the expedition left the mouth of the Kansas River and headed north.

His descriptions of this part of Kansas made it sound like a near-paradise, and he commented several times on the "raspberries purple, ripe, and abundant."

On July 3, the expedition camped somewhere around this area; the exact location isn't known, but Clark's entry for July 4 noted that they had passed the remains of a French fort, Fort de Cavagnial, which was about five miles north of present-day Fort Leavenworth. The French left in 1764, and the exact location of their fort has never been identified; perhaps it has disappeared into the river, as the channel has changed there. The Kansa Indians also had a village near the French fort.

Clark's notes for July 4, which was spent near present-day Atchison, conclude, "So magnificent a scenery in a country this situated far removed from the civilized world to be enjoyed by nothing but the buffalo, elk, deer, and bear in which it abounds, and savage Indians." Historian Stephen E. Ambrose, in his best-selling book about the expedition, *Undaunted Courage*, notes wryly, "Possibly the captains puzzled over why God had created such a place and failed to put Virginians in it, or put it in Virginia."

As for the so-called savage Indians, Lewis and Clark were 640 miles up the Missouri River, well into Nebraska, before they ever saw an Indian. As they came up this stretch of the river, all the Indians were away hunting buffalo.

Leavenworth is among the northeast Kansas communities planning festivities in 2004 to celebrate the 200th anniversary of the Lewis and Clark Expedition. For more information, contact the Convention and Visitors Bureau, listed at the end of this chapter.

Fort Museum

Backtrack to the Frontier Army Museum. This unassuming building is a gold mine of historical artifacts. Displays trace the

Human history

The Kansa Indians, for whom the state of Kansas is named, lived along the Missouri River at least as far back as the 1730s. They lived in large grass or brush lodges in villages along streams. The men were excellent fishermen, and the women gardened. During the summer, the people left the village to hunt buffalo on the plains.

By 1800, the Kansa had started to migrate west and settle along the Kansas River as far west as Fort Riley. In 1847, when the U.S. government decided it wanted to open the territory to white settlement, the Kansa Indians were relocated to a reservation near Council Grove. In 1873, they were moved again, to a reservation in Oklahoma.

President Abraham Lincoln established the National Cemetery at Fort Leavenworth.

history of the Fort, explaining its role first as a frontier post to protect trade and settlement and later as a rear-supply depot area into which supplies were funneled from the east before being sent westward to supply the growing military presence.

The museum houses the largest collection of horse-drawn vehicles in the country, including Conestoga wagons, prairie schooners, military ambulances, and stagecoaches from 1817 to 1917. Also here is the stagecoach President Abraham Lincoln used when he visited Kansas in December 1859 to see firsthand the result of the popular sovereignty experiment, in which Kansans voted in October 1859 to enter the Union as a free state.

Visit the gallery dedicated to the Buffalo Soldiers, the two black cavalry units based at Fort Leavenworth to defend the frontier. African-Americans played an important role in the military history of the United States, a role largely overlooked until the 1990s.

When you've finished at the museum, drive through the rest of the fort. Stop at the Oregon and Santa Fe Trails site, where thousands of wagons pulled supplies from the river below up the hill to the fort, leaving deep tracks that remain as evidence of the fort's role in supplying the West.

Drive past headquarters and the nearby streets lined with stately old houses that are home to the many full colonels based here. Fort Leavenworth offers nearly every amenity an officer could want, from the commissary with its low prices, to the officers' club with its swimming pool and golf course.

Be sure to visit the National Cemetery, one of 12 established in 1862 by President Lincoln. The 20,000 dead buried here were veterans of every U.S. war since the War of 1812. The oldest graves are in the center of the cemetery, near the flagpole, and they include the remains of Henry Leavenworth, a dozen Native Americans, and seven Confederate soldiers who died while being held here during the Civil War.

On the north end of the fort is the only feature that doesn't fit the prevailing image of affluence—the U.S. Disciplinary Barracks, a walled and razor-wired complex. The Disciplinary Barracks is a maximum-security prison for male and female offenders from all branches of the military. About 1,000 inmates are housed there, serving sentences that range from one day to life.

The Buffalo Soldier monument, which was created at the behest of General Colin Powell, is well worth a stop as you return to the fort's gates on your way out. The Buffalo Soldier monument, dedicated in 1992, honors the 9th and 10th Cavalry, the African-American units once based here. As the Buffalo Soldier gallery in the museum explained, these units protected civilians and played an important role in the taming of the West.

U.S. Penitentiary

Leaving the Fort, turn right on U.S. 73 and go a half mile to the U. S. Penitentiary. If you've never seen it, you will be amazed at the building's grandeur.

The War Department deeded the land on which it sits to the Justice Department in 1897; inmates from the U.S. Disciplinary Barracks at the fort provided the labor to start the construction. The first cell house opened in 1906, and the penitentiary was com-

The Buffalo Soldiers monument at Fort Leavenworth includes a sculpture and waterfall.

pleted in the mid-1920s. It's the largest maximum security prison in the United States, with 2,300 inmates, and has housed such infamous convicts as George "Machine Gun" Kelly, "Bugs" Moran, and Robert Stroud, the Bird Man of Alcatraz.

Just past the main building you will see a small herd of bison in a field. Turn right on Fort Riley Boulevard, Leavenworth County Route 14. There's a parking area where you can pull off and take a better look at the prison if you wish. Then, continue north on Route 14.

You will quickly find yourself winding through valleys and up hills that are the result of glaciation some 600,000 years ago. A huge sheet of ice covered most of the Mississippi Valley, extending as far south in Kansas as the Kaw River and as far west as the Big Blue River near Manhattan. As the glacier moved, it dragged rocks from the north and ground them into fine particles.

When the glacier receded, it dropped its load of sediment.

Winds whipped up the soil and deposited the fine dust over most of Kansas. These glacial deposits, known as loess, are more than 100 feet thick in some areas of this corner of the state. The mineral-rich loess makes for excellent farming, but the land is highly erodible because of the steep slopes. Conservation-minded farmers grow their crops on terraces that step down the hillsides, reducing the amount of soil that runs off in a rain.

Downtown Leavenworth

Backtrack to U.S. 73, and head south to downtown Leavenworth. The main commercial street is Delaware, and here you will find an abundance of restored nineteenth-century buildings. There are several good locally owned restaurants on this street, too, if you're ready for lunch. On the east end of Delaware, you will encounter the Riverfront Community Center, housed in the restored 1888 Union Pacific Train Depot. The depot is used as meeting space and as a public recreation and fitness facility.

South of the depot is the Leavenworth Landing Park, a great place to stretch your legs and study the Missouri River. Your children will enjoy the winding sidewalk, brick patterned walkways, and sculptures that invite climbing. The city plans to restore an old carousel and install it in this area.

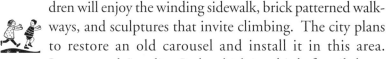

Leavenworth Landing Park, which is a third of a mile long, is an example of how a riverfront can be reclaimed from industrial use and turned into a tourist attraction and public space, something cities on the Kaw River are just beginning to recognize.

For more information

♪ Leavenworth Convention & Visitors Bureau, 518 Shawnee Street, P.O. Box 44, Leavenworth, KS 66048; 913-682-4113 or 800-844-4114.

Bonner Springs to Kansas City, Kansas

This tour takes you to several museums that provide a good perspective on the Native American and white settlement history of the Kaw Valley. Because most destinations are indoors, it is a good trip for a cold or rainy day. No special shoes or clothing are suggested.

National Agricultural Center

So much of Kansas history is interwoven with farming that brushing up on your farm knowledge is a good idea before you begin your forays into the Kaw Valley. That is one reason this tour begins at the National Agricultural Center and Hall of Fame in Bonner Springs, which was chartered by Congress to honor America's farmers. The National Agricultural Center is closed in winter, from December 1 through mid-March, but otherwise is open seven days a week.

When arriving at the center, you will notice immediately a field full of telephone poles. The Agricultural Center is home to the International Lineman's Rodeo, an annual event in which hundreds of power company linemen from all over the world compete in events based on traditional lineman tasks. In one event, the linemen must climb a utility pole while carrying an egg in a metal bucket, hang the bucket at the top, and climb back down with the egg in his or her teeth. The rodeo, open to the public, is in September; check with the Agricultural Center (the phone number is at the end of this chapter) for this year's date.

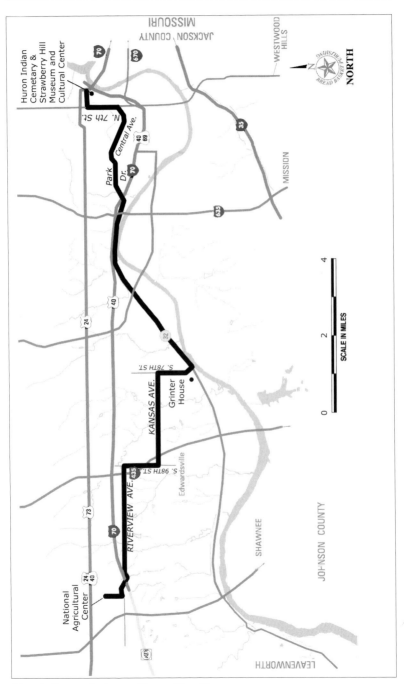

Tour 2: Bonner Springs to Kansas City, Kansas.

Inside the museum, you will find extensive exhibits about farming and rural life, including a large collection of machinery and implements of all vintages.

Outside is a reconstructed 1900-era town, which includes a one-room school house, country store, veterinarian's office, and other period buildings. You can take a ride on a narrow-gauge railroad and tour an 1887 train depot. Be sure to pick up a brochure about special events; the Agricultural Center has a number of celebrations you might want to attend with your children, such as the Prairie Winds Kite Festival and Ice Cream Days. The center also offers educational programs for classes and groups that you can schedule in advance.

Wyandotte County Museum

Just across the road from the Agricultural Center is the beautiful Wyandotte County Park, a great place for a picnic or a stretch. The park's drives are lined with pin oak trees; their perfect pyramidal shape and red autumn foliage make this variety a favorite of landscapers throughout the nation.

Within the park is the county historical society's museum, which focuses on the Native American history of the area. The museum does a good job of presenting the big picture about the Indian tribes that lived or were settled in the Kansas City area.

The oldest artifacts are from the Hopewell, people who moved to what is now Kansas City around 1 A.D. and remained here until their culture waned for unknown reasons around 700 A.D. The Hopewell buried their dead in limestone vaults, surrounded by art objects they made from copper, pipestone, obsidian, and mica gathered throughout North America. The limestone vaults were then covered with earth, making burial mounds. Many were located on the river bluffs, and as the river has shifted over the centuries, some of these burial mounds have been exposed while others have ended up in what are now residential areas far from the river.

Most items in this museum were found by an amateur archaeologist, who dug up his own backyard and many of his neighbors' backyards a few miles from here in search of these prehistoric items.

Hills and valleys

As you leave the park, turn left (east) on Riverview Road. The road is narrow and hilly, and you will travel past a mixture of old farms and new suburban-style houses as the road climbs and dips through the numerous creek valleys that wind through this area.

White Arrivals and American Indians

Two groups of Indians—the native tribes and the emigrant tribes—have lived in the Kaw Valley since white explorers arrived. Native tribes lived here long before white settlers arrived; the Kansa (see also pages 15, 108, 155), for whom the state and river were named, are believed to have moved to the Kaw Valley before 1730.

For years, the Kansa was the only tribe living in the Kaw Valley, although the Osage from the south and Pawnee from the north sometimes traveled in the area. Then in 1830, the Indian Removal Act forced the uprooting of nearly 11,000 Indians from their homes in the East. They were taken to reserves west of what was then known as the Permanent Frontier, in what is now Kansas, Missouri, and Oklahoma.

The Shawnee, from Missouri and Ohio, were the first group to arrive in Kansas, around 1826. They occupied land north and south of the Kaw. The Delaware arrived next, in 1829, and were settled north of the Kaw. They were widely known for their skill as hunters and trappers and were the only tribe that had ranged the breadth of the continent. A Delaware scout, Black Beaver, led some of the most famous expeditions west, including the journeys of John Fremont and John J. Audubon.

In 1843, the Wyandot nation arrived from Upper Sandusky, Ohio, where they had lived in a permanent village

On a few hilltops, you can see the skyline of Kansas City, Missouri, straight ahead of you, but this road still has a rural feel to it.

Perhaps you came to Bonner Springs on Interstate 70. Kansas was the first state to complete its section of I-70 when the road was built in the 1960s, but you have to wonder if the interstate ultimately worked to the detriment of Kansas's image. That flat, smooth ribbon of concrete gives little indication of the landscape it is tra-

with a sawmill, gristmill, frame and stone houses, frame and log barns, and cultivated fields. The Wyandot had intermarried with whites in Ohio for so long that there were no full-blooded Indians in the group when they were uprooted, and many were Methodists.

When they left for Indian Territory, the Wyandot were expecting a village to be ready for them, but instead they were dropped on the Kaw floodplain with no houses or tents. It was a cool, wet June when they arrived, and many Wyandot fell ill from exposure and disease. By August, more than 200 had died. To get away from their official reserve, they bought land from the Delaware in the eastern part of the county and started building, first a Methodist church, then a school. Eventually they platted the town of Wyandot, which became the heart of Kansas City, Kansas.

In the 1840s, everyone in the nation was hotly debating slavery, and the Wyandot were no exception. There were some who vehemently opposed slavery, and some who favored slavery. The issue came to head in 1847 when a Wyandot named William Walker went to Harrisonville, Missouri, and came back with a slave he had purchased there. The community was torn apart, and eventually the anti-slavery Wyandots moved north and established their own settlement of Quindaro, with the help of the New England Emigrant Aid Company, an abolitionist group that was also instrumental in the settling of Lawrence and Topeka.

versing and probably leads coast-to-coast travelers to think that Kansas is flat from one border to the other. The back road you are on now generally is less than a mile from I-70 or Interstate 435, but it allows you to see what the landscape is really like. It is not flat, and it is not bare.

In fact, the plant life in this part of Kansas is not much different from everything east, all the way to the Atlantic seaboard. The woodlands here are part of the floristic province known as the Eastern Deciduous Forest. Right now, you are close to the western edge of this province; westward, forests become smaller and more patchy, interspersed with prairie. Near Topeka, the Eastern Deciduous Forest has all but disappeared, replaced by grasslands, scrubby areas that have been invaded by trees, and lowland forests along the rivers and streams. The change in scenery is a function of rainfall: Rainfall here averages 36 inches per year; at Junction City, 120 miles west and at the start of the Kansas River Valley, rainfall is only 30 inches a year.

Transition areas between major habitats such as forest and prairie are biologically rich because many different types of plants and animals find their niches. Kansas, as a whole, has an amazing diversity of wildlife: 3,500 species of plant, 25,000 kinds of insect, and 700 kinds of other animal.

Grinter House

When the road dead-ends at 98th Street, turn right, then go left on Kansas Avenue and right on 78th Street. As you descend the hill, watch for Grinter Chapel on the right. This Methodist church was built in 1868 on land donated by Moses and Anna Grinter, whose house you are going to visit. The Grinters are buried in the cemetery there.

Moses Grinter built the handsome brick house overlooking the Kaw around 1860. A Kentucky native, Grinter arrived here at the Delaware Indian Reserve shortly after the Indians arrived. It is not known exactly what brought him. The land was not open to white settlement at that point, so he couldn't have come to stake a claim. It is thought that he might have been an Indian agent who

The Grinter House overlooks the Kaw from a hill in Wyandotte County.

came with a group of Delaware, or perhaps that he was in the military at Fort Leavenworth and sent down to help establish a military supply road to the Santa Fe Trail.

In any case, Grinter began operating a ferry at this site in 1831, and he built a cabin near the landing. Five years later, he married Anna Marshall, the daughter of a Delaware woman and a white trader. Moses and Anna had 10 children, but five died in childhood. In the 1840s, Grinter opened a trading post, and reportedly was generous about extending credit to his Delaware neighbors. Many immigrants to Oregon and California crossed the Kaw here in the 1840s and early 1850s, and the ferry was important to development of the military road that moved supplies from Fort Leavenworth to Fort Gibson, Oklahoma.

Besides running the ferry and the trading post, the Grinters farmed. They kept livestock and poultry, raised grains and vegetables, and had 400 apple trees, planted between the house and the river. In the 1880 census, the Grinter family reported owning 700 acres. By the 1860s, the railroads had arrived and built a line along the river's edge on land purchased from the Delaware. In 1866, the Delaware were moved to Oklahoma; 20 adults, including Anna, chose to remain here, which meant they had to give up their tribal rights and become U.S. citizens.

Moses operated the ferry until the 1870s, and he died in 1878. Anna lived in the house until her death in 1905, and the house remained in the Grinter family until 1950, when a Nebraska couple bought it, renovated it, and opened the popular Grinter House restaurant. In 1971, the state acquired it and began to manage it as the historic site you are visiting today.

Along the Kaw

The ferry was thought to have been just a few hundred feet down river from the Grinter House, at a place where the river bottom is rock and more easily crossed. We will head east on Kansas 32, adjacent to the river. Stay to the right, and take the Kaw Drive turnoff rather than getting back on the interstate. At this point, you are just a few miles from where the Kaw empties into the Missouri River, but this tour isn't going to take you there. At this writing, it is not worth a visit; it is an industrial area. The Lewis and Clark Viaduct, which spans the rivers' confluence, provides in its name the only nod to the historical event that is one of the most-recounted stories of the famed expedition.

Today, a person driving past the industries, cheap stores, railroad sidings, landfills, and miscellaneous junk that crowd the banks and bluffs of the Kaw near its end would have to wonder about the lack of reverence humans have had for rivers the past 150 years. People obviously understood the life-sustaining nature of rivers—after all, they built most of their communities beside them—but they also heedlessly fouled them, under the assumption that the river would carry the filth away.

Water quality

By this point in the river's course, the Kaw has received the sewage, wastewater, and runoff from 60,000 square miles of human activity. The pollutants that flow into the river come from two categories: the "point sources" that are identified and regulated, such as sewage treatment plants and industries, and the "non-point sources," which are much more problematic.

Non-point source pollution comes from many, many places: oil from city streets, pesticides from farm fields, manure from cattle pastures, overflow from failing septic systems, fertilizers from parks and suburban lawns. In addition, a great deal of erosion from farm

Lewis and Clark at the confluence

Meriwether Lewis and William Clark, on their expedition to the Pacific Ocean, spent four days camping at the mouth of the Kaw in June 1804. Here, the party reorganized as the river turned north, and the travelers prepared themselves for entry into land that was little explored and somewhat feared by Europeans. After three days of resting and repacking, the group prepared to set off the next morning. But that night, two privates who were on guard duty broke into the group's supply of whiskey and got drunk.

Clark ordered a court martial for the two young men. They were found guilty, and one was sentenced to 100 lashes on his bare back, the other to 50 lashes, and both men were flogged. The discipline was painful to set an example for the rest of the crew, but not so extreme that Lewis and Clark lost any help on their journey.

The Lewis journals for that summer have never been located, so we don't know what natural features were new and interesting to him as he explored the area around the Kaw. Clark, however, noted in his journal "the country about the mouth of this river is very fine." He recorded the width of the Kaw as 230 feet at its mouth and the width of the Missouri River as 500 feet. He weighed the water from the Kaw and Missouri rivers and found the Missouri River water to be heavier, meaning muddier. But Clark commented on the disagreeable flavor of the Kaw water.

fields and stream banks adds to the sediment load of the river. Is it any wonder the Kaw looks so muddy?

Although the Kansas River probably was never crystal-clear, because of the way it cuts into the land during times of high flow, it was not always this brown. Several explorers who came through Kansas in the 1800s commented on the clarity of the Kaw, especially in relation to the muddy Missouri. Several species of animals that once lived in the Kaw, such as the black sandshell mussel and two species of gill-breathing snails, are now gone because they can't survive in turbid water. Another species, the hickorynut mussel, was extirpated before 1900.

The pollution of the Kansas River, then, began soon after white settlement. In 1887, the Army quartermaster at Fort Riley wrote about the need to find a drinking water supply other than the Kaw.

"It is one of the nastiest rivers I know of, being the natural sewer of an immense agricultural district, flowing for hundreds of miles in an alluvial bottom and draining innumerable pig farms," he wrote. "One can stand on the bank and see, almost any day, dead animals floating down."

By the turn of the century, laws had been passed making it illegal to dump dead animals in the river. Then municipal sewage and industry became the primary threats in the Kaw and every other river in the country.

In 1972, Congress passed the Clean Water Act and ordered the states to clean up their rivers and lakes to be swimmable and fishable. The states were required to establish standards for various types of pollutants, which Kansas did. But in the late 1990s, American Rivers, a national environmental organization, still considered the Kaw one of the 20 most endangered rivers in the nation. State officials dispute that designation, saying that Kansas standards are more stringent than those of many other states, so the Kaw looks worse on paper than rivers in states with lesser standards.

In any case, the Kaw has not achieved the "fishable and swimmable" standard. The biggest pollutant in the Kansas River is fecal

Automobile batteries are among trash that people discard in the Kaw.

coliform bacteria (FCB). FCB are ubiquitous bacteria that can indicate the presence of pathogenic bacteria such as health-threaten-
ing strains of E. coli. The standard for "secondary contact" recreation, such as boating and wading, is 2,000 colonies of FCB per
100 milliliters of water; in 1998, the most recent year reported,
the entire Kansas River was too polluted for secondary contact
recreation. The standard for swimming is much tougher, and the
Kaw is far out of compliance with that standard. You definitely
don't want to risk swimming in it.

    The river isn't safe for fishing, either, because the insecticide
chlordane has been found in the tissue of Kaw River fish. Thirty
years ago, chlordane was widely used to kill termites and agricultural crop pests. Then it was discovered to be a carcinogen and
neurological poison, and in 1988 the Environmental Protection
Agency banned it. That means the chlordane showing up in the
river today is a legacy of its use more than 14 years ago. It continues to be a threat because it is bound to the sediments on the bottom of the river where invertebrates come in contact with it. In a
classic example of how the food chain concentrates pollutants, in-

vertebrates feeding on the bottom are eaten by small fish, which are eaten by bigger fish, and so on until birds or humans catch the fish, which now have significant amounts of chlordane in their tissues. That is one food chain where you don't want to be on top.

State and federal efforts to clean up our rivers are ongoing. In Kansas, the point sources of water pollution are regulated. For example, several sewage treatment plants that were releasing too much fecal coliform bacteria are now required to treat waste with chlorine to kill the bacteria before discharging the waste water into the river. Topeka's sewage treatment plant, one of the worst offenders in the past, started disinfecting its effluent in the spring of 2001, and the FCB pollution levels are now dramatically lower downstream at Lecompton.

Non-point source pollution, however, is not easily controlled. For many years, most states just ignored it on the theory that it was coming from everywhere and could not be controlled. But these non-point sources are major contributors of water pollution, so environmental groups throughout the United States have gone to court to force states to deal with the problem. That happened in Kansas, and a federal court ordered the state Department of Health and Environment to come up with a plan for reducing non-point source pollution.

So far, the state is trying to solve the problem by educational efforts and closer oversight of septic systems, among other strategies. Telling people what they can and cannot do on their own property is always a delicate issue, though, so it is politically difficult for the state to resolve the water quality problem.

Kansas City, Kansas

Kaw Drive turns into Park Drive; stay on it and follow it to Central Avenue in Kansas City, Kansas. Turn right on Central, then left on Seventh. You are now in downtown KCK, and the area known as Strawberry Hill is to your right. Just past the Wyandotte County Courthouse, on the right, is the Huron Indian Cemetery. There are a few spaces on the street where you can park for a visit to the cemetery. Bronze plaques at the entrance explain the history of the Wyandot, who were also known as the Huron, and small plaques on the graves show where many were buried after losing their lives during the relocation to this area. It is a somber place, appropriate for contemplating the fate of the once-powerful Wyandot people.

After leaving the cemetery, continue north on Seventh Street, turn right on Minnesota, then right on Fourth Street. On your right, in a big Queen Anne style house, is the Strawberry Hill Museum and Cultural Center. The house was built in 1887 and sold in 1919 to St. John the Baptist Catholic Church next door. The church used it as an orphanage for 70 years, adding a dormitory in 1926.

The museum celebrates the immigrants who moved to KCK in the early 1900s—first the Irish, Germans and Swedes, then, later, the Croats and Slavs. There is a movement within the community to revitalize the entire area from Fourth to Seventh Street between Minnesota and Central avenues. Although most houses in the area are modest by contemporary standards, the area is rich in cultural history and a wonderful example of the American melting pot where cultures from all over the world came together. At this writing, the museum is open only on weekends, but call to find out current hours.

For more information

- ✔ National Agricultural Center and Hall of Fame, 630 N. 126th St., Bonner Springs, KS 66012; 913-721-1075; www.aghalloffame. com.
- ✔ Wyandotte County Historical Museum, 631 N. 126th St., Bonner Springs, KS 66012; 913-721-1078.
- ✔ Grinter House, 1420 S. 78th St., Kansas City, KS 66111; 913-299-0373.
- ✔ Kansas City, Kansas, Chamber of Commerce information line, 800-264-1563.
- ✔ Strawberry Hill Museum, 720 N. Fourth St., Kansas City, KS 66101; 913-371-3264.

Johnson County

This tour will take you to several urban-edge parks and museums and will focus on the interaction of humans and the environment. It involves walking on paved paths, so it's not too strenuous. This one isn't a loop, and you can visit the sites in any order that makes sense for you.

Shawnee Mission Park

Begin at the main entrance to the park, near West 79th Street and Renner Road in Shawnee. This popular park is 1,250 acres and is used for many recreational activities, ranging from nature hikes to tennis to theater. We're going to drive around the park, just to appreciate its size and diversity, then head for one of the prettiest natural areas in the county.

When you arrive at the park, stop in the visitor center for a map, then follow the road that skirts the south side of the lake. Climb the observation tower to get a quick insight into the importance of this park. As far as the eye can see to the south and east, Johnson County is densely developed, and the bulldozers and skeletal buildings at the park's perimeter prove that the area's growth continues. The park is an island of green in a sea of buildings.

The fortunate vision of some residents 50 years ago saved this valley. In the 1950s, as suburban development boomed, a group of Johnson County residents realized that they needed to set aside some land for parks. At the time, though, Kansas law did not provide for local or regional park districts, so there was no taxing

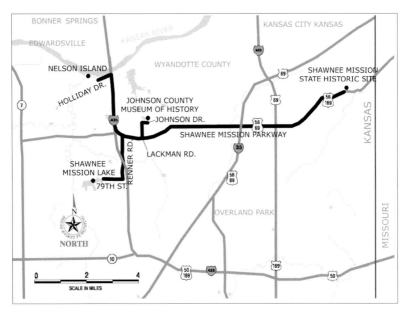

Tour 3: Johnson County.

authority that could purchase land for parks. Johnson Countians went to the Legislature, got a statute passed to establish a countywide park district, and persuaded voters to approve taxes and bonds for parks. In 1956, the land for Shawnee Mission Park was purchased, and construction of the park's dam began. In 1962, the park was dedicated.

At first, people complained that it was too far west from the populated areas of the county, but the suburbs quickly grew to meet it. Since its start, the Johnson County Park and Recreation District has added an additional 4,000 acres of parks that attract 7 million visitors a year.

Streamway parks

Park at the Streamway Park trail access on the south side of the dam, across from Shelter 8. Mill Creek Streamway Park, the largest of Johnson County's streamway parks, has 17 miles of paved trails for walking or bicycling. It extends from the Kansas River to Olathe. We're going to take a two-mile stroll along Mill Creek to introduce you to the streamway park concept.

In 1986, voters approved this new approach to parks, in which land along streams is acquired for natural areas. Streamway parks serve a number of useful purposes. They provide quiet, shady places in picturesque areas where people can walk or ride bicycles. They offer uninterrupted stretches of habitat for animals that live in riparian (or water-bank) areas or along the edges of these areas, so that the animals can move about freely without having to risk their lives in traffic.

Also, riparian areas serve as sponges that soak up extra rainfall and deter flooding. If they get paved over, flooding downstream worsens. By preserving the floodplain as parkland, flood damage is minimized. A low-impact streamway park such as this one, with nothing more than a bike path and occasional benches, lets water rise and fall at nature's whim, with nothing harmed.

Hike down through the woods, which are typical second-growth oak-hickory forest. Although there are some remnants of virgin forest in eastern Kansas, identifiable by their huge trees, most native trees were cut early in the years of white settlement, and those that are here today are 100 to 150 years old at most. In eastern Kansas, there are two kinds of forests: riparian and upland. Riparian forests are those that cover the valleys carved by rivers and streams. Cottonwood, green ash, and elm trees dominate these forests. Upland forests, away from floodplains, are dominated by oaks and hickories.

Oaks are the most prevalent type of tree in eastern Kansas. The state has 11 distinct oak species; they're divided into two categories, the black oaks and white oaks. Black oaks have bristle-tipped lobes on their leaves, and their acorns take two years to mature. Red oaks and blackjack oaks are in this category. White oaks have leaves with rounded lobes and produce an acorn crop every year. The most widely distributed white oak is the bur oak, which can grow to 90 feet and live 450 years. The bur oaks are easily identified in fall by their big acorns with fringed caps.

The most common hickory is the shagbark hickory, so named because its bark naturally breaks into strips that curl outward, giving it a shaggy look. They are easy to spot as you walk through the upland woods.

At the bottom of the hill, when the trail forks, go left. We're going to make a loop around the big field in front of you, formerly a cultivated field that is now a brome hay field. The path follows Mill Creek around a curve. Soon the drone of the interstate highway to the south will fade, and you will be able to hear the fast-moving creek splashing over rock ledges.

Mill Creek is only a few inches deep in most parts because its limestone bottom has resisted erosion, but occasionally you will come to a deep pool. Though it may look like a swimming or fishing hole, resist the temptation. Contact with the water is not recommended. Like most urban streams, Mill Creek is polluted. This particular section is also remarkably free of meanders, thanks

A riparian area flanks Mill Creek, a shallow but swift stream.

to the railroad, which straightened the creek's channel in the 1940s to protect the adjacent railroad tracks.

Along the streamway path, watch for the Kansas champion hackberry tree, which is marked with a small plaque. With a circumference of 13 feet, 8 inches, and a height of more than 68 feet, this is the biggest hackberry tree in the state — at least until someone finds a bigger one and nominates it to the Kansas State Division of Forestry, which is the judge of such matters.

Notice the picturesque bridges on this path; they are called pony truss bridges and were built in the early 1900s and used on county roads. These two were slated for demolition because they had outlived their usefulness for car traffic, but the park district recycled them for pedestrians and bicycles.

You will also see some remnants of the farm that was once here, including the stone foundation of a barn. Another highlight of this walk is the man-made wetland, which is attractive to waterfowl and migratory birds. Keep your eyes open, and you will see all kinds of avian life cavorting in this border between the open field and the riparian area.

Bluebirds

The most obvious signs of birds are the many bluebird boxes. Shawnee Mission Park is the state-decreed "Bluebird Capital of Kansas," thanks to the efforts of park staff and volunteers. There are 200 bluebird boxes in the park and along Mill Creek, and the success rate has been impressive. More than 1,000 baby bluebirds fledge from these boxes most years.

You will hear their soft warble and catch the flash of blue as they flit from nest boxes into the trees. If you're attentive, you may even see a few youngsters learning to fly. These are Eastern bluebirds, one of three species of bluebirds found in the United States. The Eastern bluebird male has an azure blue back and rust breast; the female is a duller version of the same colors. The young are spotted with blue or bluish-gray tail and wing feathers.

Bluebirds have an esteemed position in our culture. Robert Frost wrote a children's poem about them, Henry David Thoreau

Bluebird boxes such as this one have helped make Shawnee Mission Park the Bluebird Capital of Kansas.

described them in his journals, and Judy Garland sang about them in "Over the Rainbow." Yet 25 years ago, Eastern bluebirds were in danger of extinction. Their numbers, which probably peaked around 1900, had plummeted 90 percent by the 1970s because of habitat loss.

Bluebirds live in open meadows surrounded by hedgerows; in this kind of environment they can easily find food. Bluebirds eat insects in spring, summer, and fall, and they prefer sparse or mowed vegetation where their prey can be easily spotted. In winter, they eat berries, including those on our native hackberry and cedar trees. Farms provided the perfect habitat for bluebirds, but as farmland gave way to suburbs, bluebirds declined.

At the same time, nest areas decreased. Bluebirds are called secondary cavity nesters, which means they can't drill their own holes for nesting but must rely on cavities that are already available. Dead trees and wooden fences provided the usual places where bluebirds nested. But as woodlands were cut down and wooden fences were replaced by metal ones, bluebirds had fewer and fewer places to nest.

To make matters worse, an exploding population of house sparrows and starlings took over the remaining nest sites. These species had been introduced from Europe in 1850 and 1890, respectively, and were well-suited to an urban environment. House sparrows and starlings are much more aggressive than bluebirds and will drive off bluebirds and even kill them on the nest and throw out the eggs.

By the mid-1970s, a movement to save the bluebird swept the country. When people learned that bluebirds would readily accept a manufactured nesting cavity, bluebird enthusiasts set to work, erecting single boxes in suburban back yards and "bluebird trails" of hundreds or even thousands of boxes in parks and on conservation land.

Opinions vary and are fervently held about the best type of box for bluebirds. The type you see here is the Peterson Bluebird House, whose advocates believe it best because the roof shields the baby birds from rain, the narrow width makes it easier for the bird to build a nest and the depth makes it harder for predators to reach in and grab the babies.

And there are plenty of bluebird predators. These boxes have mesh around the nest hole to prevent cats and raccoons from reaching in to the birds, and pole guards to keep snakes from climbing up to the nests. The biggest threat to bluebirds is still the house sparrow, and volunteers make the rounds of these boxes at least once a week in spring to clean out sparrow nests, which are distinguishable from bluebird nests because sparrows' nests are messy and bluebirds' nests are neat and orderly.

Bluebirds usually arrive in this area in early March and start nesting. The clutches are usually three to five sky blue eggs. A pair may have two or even three broods per summer if the weather is good. In fall, bluebirds gather into flocks of 20 or more and travel together on their migration south. In mild winters, they may be seen here all year long.

Johnson County Museum of History

After completing your walk, follow the map to the nearby

Hackberry tree

Hackberry trees are not especially popular for landscaping these days, probably because they have bark that is often described as "warty" and have dull yellow fall foliage. A number of pests and diseases plague them. A fungus causes the trees to develop "witches brooms," dense clusters of deformed twigs along the branches. Hackberry trees are host to hackberry butterflies, which emerge in huge numbers in summer. Some people are charmed by this butterfly's habit of landing on humans and sticking there, but others find it a bit too forward.

Despite its shortcomings, the hackberry is a stalwart native of the Midwest. It grows along streams and in uplands, tolerates drought and wind, and grows quickly to a fine shape, much like the beloved but fast disappearing American Elm to which it is related. It produces berries that ripen in fall and hang on all winter, providing an important source of food for many birds. The berries are said to taste like dates, but be

careful if you try one - the seed inside is so hard it can shatter your teeth. The hackberry is a good place to look for the brilliant orange-and-black oriole, which often hang their sac-like nests in the pendulous branches.

A towering hackberry tree.

Johnson County Museum of History at Lackman Road and 63rd Street. If Shawnee Mission Park gave you an inkling of the natural beauty of this area, the museum will elaborate.

Johnson County started out prairie turned to farm country, and the county retained farming as a primary occupation until after World War II. In the western part of the county, you can still see farm remnants, and, in fact, two thirds of Johnson County's 476 square miles are still undeveloped. But as you travel east into the older suburbs and particularly along the I-35 corridor, the houses and highways increasingly conceal the native landscape until it becomes hard to imagine that there were once peach orchards, dairy farms, and spinach fields here.

The museum's main exhibit explores what "the good life" has meant for residents of Johnson County—from the Shawnee Indians who moved here believing the government's promise that this would be a permanent home, to the white settlers who established farms, to the city dwellers who fled urban problems in search of a wholesome suburban life. To their credit, the Johnson County historians don't gloss over the ugly parts of that search for the "good life," which included removing the Shawnee to Oklahoma and barring African-Americans and Jews from many housing developments.

The museum has excellent photo exhibits, and you can easily spend an hour here. You may also want to visit the all-electric home out back, if you're young enough not to be unnerved by the idea that a 1950s trend is now considered history.

Shawnee Indian Mission

The next stop is the Shawnee Indian Mission State Historic Site at 3402 W. 53rd St. in Fairway. Here you will find three brick buildings that were part of a Methodist mission school to the Shawnee before Kansas became a territory and the United States removed the Indians.

The mission played an important role in western expansion during the first half of the 19th century. Beginning in the 1820s, the Shawnee agreed to give up their land in Ohio and southeastern Missouri and move to Indian Territory, west of the Missouri River.

Thanks to early explorers such as Zebulon Pike, who found little to recommend Kansas, white Americans thought of this area as the "Great American Desert" and granted the Shawnee a generous 1.6 million acres. Church groups, intent on bringing Christianity to the Indians, established missionary programs for the newly formed reservation.

The first to arrive were the Methodists, headed by the Rev. Thomas Johnson and his wife, Sarah Johnson, for whom the county is named. They built a two-story log school north of the Kansas River in what is now Turner, and the school boarded both Shawnee and Delaware children.

Baptists and Society of Friends (Quakers) also established missions nearby, and a rivalry developed among the three sects to win converts to their particular brands of Christianity. The Baptists promoted a "new system" of education—teaching Indian children in their own language. The Methodists insisted on teaching in English, because they believed that using the Indians' language impeded efforts to "civilize" them. But the Shawnee responded so

The west building at the Shawnee Indian Mission site is the oldest. It was used for classrooms and for housing teachers.

favorably to the use of their language that the Methodists eventually were forced to accept it.

Another division among the denominations arose over boarding schools: The Baptists refused to support the expensive schools, but the Methodists believed they would win over Indian children more quickly by removing them from their parents. The Indians, who were living in poverty, agreed to send their children to boarding school so that they could be fed and clothed.

Although many Shawnee clung to their semi-nomadic traditional ways after moving to Indian Territory, with each passing year they had more difficulty finding wild game for food and eventually acquiesced to the white missionaries' attempts to have them settle and farm. By 1850, after 200 years of living near white people, there were few full-blood Shawnee, and the influence of white parents had made many people more amenable to white ways.

To expedite the transition to a farming culture, the ambitious Reverend Johnson persuaded his church to establish a large manual labor school open to Indians of all tribes. A site was selected near the Santa Fe Trail, and in 1839 the Indians agreed to let Johnson have all the land he needed for his school and farm.

In the next two years, three large brick buildings, which still stand, were erected here for classrooms, chapel, and dormitories. At the height of activity, the school had 16 buildings, 2,000 acres, and 200 Indian children ages 5 to 23. In addition to religion and academics, boys were taught farming, blacksmithing, and wagonmaking; girls were taught spinning, weaving, cooking, and domestic chores.

The mission school may have succeeded in making farmers of the Shawnee, but it is questionable how successful the Reverend Johnson was in winning converts to Christianity. Spirituality was an integral part of Shawnee life, and most were not willing to abandon it for white missionaries' religious beliefs. In an 1846 census, the Indian agent estimated that three fourths of the tribe adhered to its traditional religion.

By 1854, the U.S. government realized that eastern Kansas was not a hostile desert but was, in fact, a place of fertile land and abundant water. Kansas became a territory, and the government made plans to force out the Indians to make way for white settlement. At the same time, the issue of whether Kansas would become a free or slave state arose, and the Shawnee mission played a role in those early days of "Bleeding Kansas." The first governor of Kansas Territory, Andrew Reeder of Pennsylvania, set up offices there. And after the first territorial legislature rebelled against its unfinished quarters at Fort Riley, it adjourned to these buildings. It was also at the Shawnee mission where the proslavery legislators, illegally elected when Missouri residents poured into Kansas on election day, passed the "Bogus Laws" that made it a crime to speak against slavery.

The manual training school ended in 1854, and the mission was closed in 1862. During the Civil War, Union troops used the buildings as quarters and a hospital. The Reverend Johnson was loyal to the Union, although he had been a lifelong supporter of slavery and, in fact, had kept slaves here at the mission. He was murdered at his home in Kansas City, Missouri, in 1865. Although the murderers were never found, it is believed that Southern sympathizers killed him because they were angry that he had not joined the Confederacy.

Nelson Island

At the northern border of Johnson County is another segment of the Mill Creek Streamway Park. Leave your car at the Wilder Road access area. This was the site of the Shawnee Indian mill, for which Mill Creek is named. The Shawnee had both a grist mill and a saw mill here. Walk along the paved trail to the north, and you will come to a bridge that leads to a small island at the edge of the Kaw River.

The island is named for Cleggie Nelson, who ran a speakeasy here during Prohibition, but then spent the rest of his life as a hermit. When Nelson took title to the island in 1920, it was 27 acres and was reached by a hanging bridge. Today, the powerful force of the river has eroded the sandy banks and diminished the island to half its former size. In the fall of 1998, the flooding

Kaw took a big chunk of the island, slicing off a quarter mile of paved path.

The island provides an excellent example of the woods that are typical of riparian areas all along the Kaw. Big cottonwood and sycamore trees, with a tangled undergrowth of shrubs and vines, line the sandy banks of the river and serve as perches for the bald eagles that winter here. A biological survey a few years ago found 75 plant species. The trail cuts through the undergrowth, giving you a shady place to walk and an opportunity to get close to the river.

Unlike the peaceful trail in Shawnee Mission Park, this area endures a constant din of urban activity. Cars and trucks roar by on Interstate 435 as it crosses the Kaw, the sand operation across the river adds its drone, and, to the south, garbage trucks and giant earth movers beep and rumble in the Johnson County landfill. Yet wildlife stills finds a home here, a testament to the resilience of nature.

Dredging

The sand operation across the river from Nelson Island is an example of a complicated issue. Sand is an important economic resource, essential in construction, but people disagree strongly over how sand should be taken.

River dredging, where sand is taken from the stream bed, is the cheapest method and requires only 10 acres of land for the processing plant. The alternative is to take the sand from pits dug on the floodplain, but pit dredging requires up to 100 acres. As a result, sand companies have preferred river dredges on this part of the river, where the floodplain is just a mile wide; in the upper reaches of the Kaw, where the floodplain is up to 4 miles wide, most sand is taken from pit dredges, which is less disruptive to the river ecology.

Kaw River sand is said to be some of the best-quality and lowest-priced sand in the United States, and the rapidly urbanizing Kaw Valley has an insatiable appetite for it. In recent years, nine river dredges have operated in the Kaw, mostly in the stretch of the river from Lawrence to Kansas City.

A dredge pulls sand from the Kansas River near Kansas City, Kansas.

Biologists, however, have found that dredging has numerous negative effects on the ecology of the river. Dredging deepens the river channel, which causes the water to flow faster, erode the banks more severely, and dissolve sandbars and sand islands upstream to fill the holes left by dredging. These sandbars and the shallows around them are the most biologically productive areas of the river. According to the Kansas Biological Survey, 75% of all the species in the river live or feed in shallow areas.

Too much dredging results in a loss of habitat for the creatures that depend on the shallows. The exposed sandbars are important to many species. Turtles lay their eggs on them, birds nest on them, raccoons forage for food on them; fewer sandbars means fewer places for these animals. In a nutshell, dredging disrupts the web of life in the river. Pit mining on the floodplain is generally considered a more environmentally sound alternative to river dredging, provided that fertile farmland isn't used and that provisions are made to protect groundwater and reclaim the land later.

Although environmental groups have pushed for a total ban on dredging in some sections of the Kaw, the Kansas Legislature has refused. Consequently, state regulators who issue dredging permits are left to balance the conflicting interests of industry and ecology.

Big bones

This stretch of the river differs from the rest of the Kaw in that the valley is narrower, so the water flows faster, and the channel floor is eroding more quickly. One result is the frequent appearance of fossils of extinct Ice Age animals that are removed from the channel floor. Canoeists regularly find chocolate-brown chunks of bones on sandbars here, and there's at least one semi-professional collector who tours the river by boat after every high-water event and collects bones to sell to museums. Some of the fossils found in this area have been quite important—mastodons, hairy mammoths, saber-toothed cat, giant beavers, and more. An exhibit in the basement of the Museum of Natural History at the University of Kansas displays some of these big river fossils.

Just west of Nelson Island, you will notice a handsome Spanish-style building along the river. It's the headquarters of Hermes Nursery, where trees and shrubs are grown in the sandy bottomland soil as well as in containers. Its specialty is big trees, and though most sales are wholesale, it does sell directly to the public.

For more information

- Shawnee Mission Park, 7900 Renner Road, Shawnee Mission, KS 66219; 913-438-7275.
- Johnson County Museum of History, 6305 Lackman Road, Shawnee, KS 66217; 913-631-6709; www.digitalhistory.com.
- Shawnee Indian Mission, 3403 W. 53rd St., Fairway, KS 66205; 913-262-0867.
- Hermes Nursery, 20000 W. 47th St., Shawnee, KS 66218; 913-441-2400.

Olathe and the Kaw bottomlands

This is a real outdoorsy trip, taking you to one living history farm, two nature hikes, and a driving tour of some of the most productive farmland on earth. Pick a beautiful day, and dress comfortably. Start in Olathe at the Mahaffie Farmstead, on Kansas City Road, northwest of the intersection of Interstate 35 and Santa Fe.

Mahaffie Farmstead and Stagecoach Stop

James and Lucinda Mahaffie moved here from Indiana in 1857 and bought 160 acres of land not far from the small settlement of Olathe, which was also founded that year. The Mahaffies were farmers, but they knew a good business opportunity when they saw one. The Santa Fe and Oregon-California trails ran right by their farmstead. And as the West developed, the stagecoach that carried mail and passengers came though several times a day. The stagecoach trip from Westport, now part of Kansas City, Missouri, to Santa Fe, New Mexico, took more than 13 days, and the stagecoaches stopped every 15 miles to change horses and every 30 miles to let passengers eat and stretch. The Mahaffies contracted with the stage company to be a stagecoach stop. Their homestead is the only one remaining today on the Santa Fe Trail.

Mrs. Mahaffie set up a kitchen and tables in the cellar of her house, and she and her six children served up to 60 travelers a day. The food came from their own farm, where they raised vegetables, fruit, corn, wheat, chickens, dairy cows, pigs, and beef cattle.

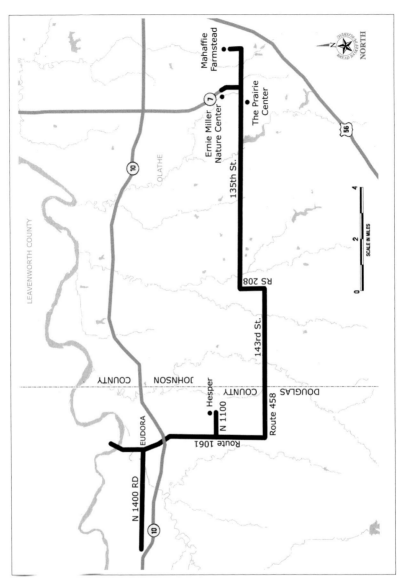

Tour 4: Olathe and the Kaw bottomlands.

The Mahaffies prospered, eventually increasing their land holdings to 570 acres and furnishing their home to reflect their wealth. By 1870, though, railroads began to replace stagecoaches, and the family no longer served travelers.

Today, you can tour the house, including the dining area in

the cellar, which is filled with period artifacts and is listed on the National Register of Historic Places. Out back, you can see a stone icehouse and wooden barn that are also on the National Register. You can see horse-drawn vehicles and farm implements typical of the period, as well as livestock breeds that might have lived here in the 1860s.

The second weekend of every month, the farm comes alive with demonstrations of farm skills such as plowing with horses, blacksmithing, butter churning, and rug-making. There are also horse-drawn stagecoach rides. Several festivals during the year--such as Civil War Days, to commemorate the border wars—focus attention on a specific aspect of the farm's history. Hours are limited during the school year, so call ahead.

Olathe

From here, drive through downtown Olathe on your way out of town. Go south on Ridgeview, and turn west on Santa Fe. The city got its name from the Shawnee word for "beautiful." Olathe was founded in 1857 by John T. Barton, a Virginia doctor appointed to serve the Shawnee whose reservation encompassed this area until Kansas was opened to white settlement in 1854.

Being so close to the Missouri border, Olathe suffered its share of attacks by border ruffians intent on making Kansas open to slavery. William Quantrill, so famous for his devastating attack on the abolitionist stronghold of Lawrence, also raided and looted Olathe.

After the Civil War, Olathe became a thriving small town, surrounded by rich farmland. At the turn of the century, a gas-electric trolley was built from Olathe to downtown Kansas City, Missouri, yet the population remained steady at 4,000 people until World War II.

The U.S. Naval Air Transport and Technical Training Unit operated here until 1970. After Interstate 35 was completed in 1957, Olathe began to grow by leaps and bounds. The population in 1960 was 10,000; today, it is 93,000 and growing. It is the seat of Johnson County government.

Ernie Miller Nature Center

Go west on Santa Fe to Kansas 7 and then north about one mile to the Ernie Miller Nature Center. The center is part of the Johnson County Parks and Recreation District and another good example of what a well-funded parks system can do. Three miles of nature trails traverse prairie and riparian areas, with guideposts keyed to an interpretive booklet that is appropriate for upper elementary children to adults. The trails are paved, and though you never quite escape the noise of the nearby highway, it is a pleasant place for a stroll.

The nature center has two resident birds, a hawk and an owl, kept in cages inside or outside the building, depending on the weather. There's a small amphitheater where experts offer presentations in the summer about wildlife and the area's cultural history. In addition, the center offers a good range of classes for children from preschool to high school age to learn about natural history.

The Prairie Center

Just west of the burgeoning commercial development of Olathe is a 300-acre natural area with six miles of trails and a 5-acre lake. From the Ernie Miller Park, backtrack a mile south to 135th street; go west three miles to the Prairie Center. The Prairie Center is owned by the Kansas Department of Wildlife and Parks and is open to the public from dawn till dusk seven days a week for hiking and fishing. The landscape here recalls the prairie of the nineteenth century.

Travelers on the Oregon and Santa Fe trails were already a day out of Kansas City when they reached Olathe. Imagine how they must have felt as they left the town behind and set off into the expansive prairie that stretched to the horizon, broken only by lines of trees along the creeks. Waving grasses, 8 to 12 feet tall, covered almost all of these uplands. Wildfires started by lightning frequently raced across the land, burning out woody vegetation and leaving blackened soil that soon sprouted a carpet of brilliant green. The prairie was a strange and somewhat frightening landscape for most of the travelers, but the promise of prosperity awaited in the Southwest, Oregon, and California.

Visitors to the Prairie Center can get a sense of the sea of grasses that met nineteenth-century pioneers.

More than a quarter million people responded to prosperity's call and passed through here between 1840 and 1870. Many others saw this area as their final destination and staked claims to the land soon after Kansas Territory was opened in 1854. A family named Lawrence was listed as the first settlers of the land where the Prairie Center now sits.

In 1913, George and Frieda Algire purchased a parcel and established a farm. Algire, a stonemason, built a house, brooder house, chicken house, garage, stone walls, and lamp posts from limestone found on the land. The first house, covered with stucco, burned in the late 1920s, and the family lived in the chicken coop until the house that stands today was completed in the 1930s. About 45 acres of the prairie were left untouched, and the rest was plowed and planted to crops. The Algires sold the farm in 1963 to R.C. Wagner and his son Larry, who wanted to restore the land to its native condition.

The Wagners protected the virgin prairie and reseeded the cropland to native species of grasses and wildflowers. They also built and stocked a 5-acre lake. In 1983, the non-profit Grassland Heritage Foundation took over management of the land and started

educational programs for the community. Ownership was transferred to the state in 1990, and extensive renovation work on the
buildings and land is under way.

Today, the Prairie Center provides plenty of opportunity for
self-guided natural recreation, plus various educational programs.
One of the biggest events of the year is the third weekend in April,
when a day of programming about the role of fire on the prairie
leads to an actual nighttime burn.

Mowed grass trails traverse the varied habitats found here:
native prairie near the farmstead and the western edge, reseeded
prairie, upland woodland and riparian areas, plus the pond. Depending on the time of year, you may see a variety of wildflowers,
birds, beaver, and deer.

Sunflower Army Ammunition Plant

As you leave the Prairie Center, continue west on 135th Street
until the road dead-ends at the old Sunflower Army Ammunition
Center. The Sunflower plant made munitions during World War
II and the Cold War, and the land here contains various types of
toxic waste that need to be cleaned up before the center can be
developed for any other purpose.

One developer's plan to build a theme park here has been
rejected, but other proposals are under consideration. Kansas State
University is developing a gardening research and demonstration
center at this end of the property, but at this writing it is not open
to the public. Watch for a public welcome center to be developed
here in the future.

For now, just turn left, then right at the next road, to skirt the
perimeter of the fenced property. Keep your eyes open for deer, as
they are abundant along this stretch of road.

Hesper Friends Community

When you reach Douglas County Route 1061, go north two
miles, and turn right (east) on N. 1100 Road. About a mile down
this road, you will come to the Hesper Friends Meeting House.
This site was once a thriving town, founded in 1858 by Quakers
who came to Kansas Territory mostly from North Carolina to lend

their votes to the free state movement. When the Civil War broke out, they were joined by other white Southerners who abhorred slavery and hoped to make a new life for themselves in a free state.

On August 21, 1863, William Quantrill and a party of border ruffians came into Kansas from Missouri, intent on revenge against abolitionists who were winning the war against slavery. They were heading for the free state stronghold of Lawrence, but, as they passed through Hesper, they stopped at several houses looking for men of fighting age. Mr. Stone, who was in the Union Army, was killed, but his adult son escaped out the back door and hid in a cornfield. After Quantrill left, the story is told, the younger Stone tried to ride to Lawrence to warn of the impending attack, but his horse broke its leg. Lawrence was caught unawares, 250 men and boys were killed, and much of the town was destroyed.

In 1884, Hesper Academy, the first secondary school in this area, opened to students of all religious beliefs. The academy became a vital center of social life for people from miles around. On the grounds, north of the present church, were tennis courts, a

The Hesper Friends Church maintains the old Hesper Academy school bell.

Pleasant, not ghostly

Hesper is one of hundreds of small Kansas communities that flourished from 1854 until the advent of the automobile, which shortened travel time and made small-town services redundant. Towns were so abundant in early Kansas that when Horace Greeley, editor of *The New York Tribune*, toured the state for the first time in 1859, he wrote, "It takes three log houses to make a city in Kansas, but they begin *calling* it a city as soon as they have staked out the lots."

Many people refer to these vestiges of communities as "ghost towns," but most are like Hesper — not at all ghostly, but rather pleasant places with one or two buildings to recall their history.

baseball diamond, and horse stables. Inside the cross-shaped school building, a walnut staircase led to a second floor hall that seated 250 people. On Friday evenings, lecturers on politics, science, and the arts would speak to full houses.

At its peak, Hesper had about 400 residents, several businesses, and a dozen homes in the village. Hesper residents fanned out through Kansas to start other Quaker congregations, including Friends University in Wichita. By the turn of the century, though, as the main thoroughfares were built farther north, Hesper began to decline. When the public high school opened in Eudora, Hesper Academy enrollment dropped, and the school graduated its last class in 1912. The land was purchased by a doctor from Kansas City, and when efforts by some residents to preserve it failed, the academy was demolished. Its bell was moved to the meeting house, where you can see it now.

The Hesper Friends Meeting is still a viable congregation and the heart of the community, which is dispersed across the countryside. The meeting house is the original church building, but it has been added to and remodeled many times. The hilltop cemetery, which has many nineteenth-century gravestones of the early religious settlers, is still tended by members of the congregation. The farmhouse barely visible through the trees west of the meeting house was built in 1866 and still serves as a home.

Kansas River bottomland

Retrace your path to Route 1061, and go north to Eudora. This town, with its modest houses and many churches, is typical of the farm communities that dot the edges of the Kansas River. Generally, a bridge across the river was the factor that determined whether a river town thrived or failed. Eudora has a bridge, and it's worth a trip over it and into the floodplain on the north side of the river to get a closer look at the sandy floodplain soil famous for its ability to grow just about anything.

From Eudora to the mouth of the river, the floodplain is less than a mile wide in most places, but from this point westward, it broadens to three and even four miles wide. Most of the floodplain is on the north side of the river, probably because most of the tributaries enter from the north and keep the main channel of the river pushed to the south of the valley it occupies.

In this area, the Wakarusa River enters from the south, and the floodplain is on both sides of the river, but the river still continues to erode and deposit, erode and deposit. Farmers on one side can lose dozens of acres from one high-water event, while those on the other side find themselves gaining land. And so it goes, back and forth. Those who have lived here all their lives understand that such are the ways of nature, but that knowledge doesn't make it any easier when 30 acres of valuable cropland suddenly disappear into the river.

Direct market farming

Turn around and come back into Eudora, then go west on North 1400 Road (Douglas County Route 442). As you drive toward Lawrence, you will see some of the most productive farmland available anywhere, although its use for agriculture is endangered. You can do your part to save local farmland by stopping at a farm that is open to the public, shopping at your local farmers' markets, and buying locally grown products whenever possible.

Bottomland bountiful

As you make these trips up and down the Kaw River Valley, you will notice that the flat floodplain is sometimes on the north of the river, as here, and sometimes on the south. In fact, the river winds and meanders through a broad, flat valley with bluffs on either side. The actual channel of the river is only part of the valley it occupies. The entire valley, carved from bedrock and filled with sediment deposited by the river, is called the floodplain or bottomland.

Before its taming by the U.S. Army Corps of Engineers, the Kaw meandered all over its floodplain, spreading out during times of high flow and depositing sediment as the water receded. The fine sediment left behind, known as alluvium, is up to 95 feet deep in the floodplain. The water table in the alluvial aquifer is just a few feet below the surface at times. This combination of sandy, well-drained soil and easy access to water for irrigation makes this some of the most desirable farmland anywhere.

Although most of this vast acreage is devoted to corn, wheat, milo, and soybeans, the crops haven't always been that way. At the turn of the century, farmers used these bottomlands primarily for "truck farming," that is, vegetable and fruit production that farmers trucked into the cities to sell.

Potatoes were the biggest crop, with 18,800 acres grown between Lecompton and DeSoto in 1925. Farmers also grew sweet potatoes, beets, tomatoes, peas, beans, pumpkins, spinach, and sweet corn. Orchards and vineyards were abundant, too. Farmers' menu of crops to take to grocery stores in Lawrence or to the City Market in Kansas City, Missouri, included apples, peaches, pears, and grapes.

In 1900, a cannery opened in east Lawrence, giving Kaw Valley farmers a ready market for their vegetables. The Kaw Valley Cannery operated until 1925, when declining prices for canned goods shut it down. In 1930, Columbus Foods purchased and re-opened the plant, and in 1950 Stokely-Van Camp bought it. The cannery continued producing canned vegetables into the 1980s, although by that time the produce was shipped in by rail.

Fruits and vegetable production in the Kaw Valley survived into the 1950s despite many challenges. Growing was never easy because of the unpredictable weather. Although eastern Kansas is an excellent place to grow horticultural crops, on average, extreme swings in the weather can ruin any given harvest. An abnormally bitter winter can kill trees, late spring freezes can ruin a budding fruit crop, and excessively hot, dry summers wreak havoc on veg-etables. State apple harvest in 1919, for example, was 1.2 million bushels; two years later, orchards harvested only 100,000 bushels. The drought of 1934-1937 killed many orchards and vineyards in the valley, but farmers who survived replanted.

Even World War II and the extreme labor shortage it caused didn't destroy the labor-intensive truck farming here. Local farm and business leaders worked with the Army to set up a prisoner-of-war camp just outside of Lawrence, and as many as 320 German POWs were moved here to work on farms, in businesses, and in construction. (Danforth Chapel on the KU campus was built by prisoners of war.) In July 1945, 175 prisoners of war harvested 1,000 acres of potatoes in this valley for 33 farmers.

The flood of 1951 was the death knell for fruit and vegetable production. The Kaw and Wakarusa rivers raged out of their banks and covered virtually all of this floodplain. Orchards died, pea-shelling barns and equipment washed away, and soil was unwork-able. As farmers recovered from the flood, many decided to try what was then a relatively new crop in the United States, soybeans. Bigger tractors introduced in the 1950s made larger-scale farming more practical, too, and farmers found they could make more money working with a tractor than doing the backbreaking physi-cal work of vegetable farming.

For a few decades after, Kaw Valley farms thrived. Fertile soil, access to water, and good prices for crops made decent livelihoods for most farmers here. But the picture today is very different. Crop

John and Karen Pendleton are among Kaw Valley farmers who have survived in part by growing and selling products--such as flowers and asparagus--direct to consumers.

prices are at their lowest in 30 years, often less than the cost of production. When that happens, farmers can no longer afford to farm. Farmers nearing retirement who have no savings are forced to sell land. Neighbors who might have bought it in years past to expand their own farms are no longer interested. So the best farmland in the state gets sold for housing and development.

At least 14 states have recognized the threat to farmland by suburban developments and have instituted Purchase of Development Rights (PDR) programs, in which farmers are paid the difference between the value of their land for farming and the value of their land for development. For example, this bottomland might be worth only $3,000 an acre for farming, but $6,000 an acre to a housing developer. A PDR program would pay the farmer $3,000 an acre to preserve the land for farming in perpetuity. Kansas does not have a PDR program.

One saving grace for this farmland may be the growth of direct marketing, in which farmers sell food directly to consumers, cutting out the middlemen and getting full retail price for their products. Dotted throughout the valley are various direct-market farms producing crops that are attractive to consumers. Examples include asparagus and greenhouse tomatoes at Pendleton's Country Market; pears, peaches, apples, and grapes at Davenport Orchards; and pumpkins at Schaake's Pumpkin Patch.

As the population in the Kansas River Valley increases, so does the market for farm-fresh food. But it's unlikely that the entire Kaw River bottomlands will ever return to production for local markets. Unless commodity prices rise to viable levels and make farming profitable again—or unless Kansans become more deliberate about preserving farmland through some kind of PDR program—this productive valley one day may become another housing development.

For more information

- Mahaffie Farmstead, 1100 Kansas City Road, Olathe, KS 66051; 913-782-6972.
- Ernie Miller Nature Center, 909 N. K-7 Highway, Olathe, KS 66061; 913-764-7759.
- The Prairie Center, 26325 135th St., Olathe, KS 66061; 913-894-9113, ext. 13.
- Pendleton's Country Market, 1446 E. 1850 Road, Lawrence, KS 66046; 785-843-1409.
- Davenport Orchards and Winery, 1394 E. 1900 Road, Eudora, KS 66025; 785-542-2278.
- Schaake's Pumpkin Patch, 1791 N. 1500 Road, Lawrence, KS 66046; 785-843-2459.

Lawrence to Baldwin

As whites settled the Kansas River Valley in the 1850s, it became a microcosm of the struggles taking place in the nation as a whole over the issue of slavery. Lawrence, in particular, was the site of some of the bloodiest skirmishes and most dramatic political actions that preceded the Civil War, and this tour will focus on that aspect of Lawrence's history. This tour will also explore the landscape around Lawrence, which begins to change from Eastern Deciduous Forest to tallgrass prairie. You will travel about 50 miles by car and get out for several easy strolls.

Brushing up on the history

Before you begin the tour, spend a few moments recalling the social and political climate of the United States in the middle of the nineteenth century. The nation was expanding westward rapidly, but the political division between North and South over slavery was deepening. Reflect on the terrible facts of slavery—the unspeakable injustice, brutality, and immorality of it—and you will put yourself into the frame of mind that brought settlers from their comfortable homes in the East to establish Lawrence on the south bank of the Kaw.

The slave vs. free state controversy had already divided the country for more than 40 years when Congress passed the Kansas-Nebraska Act in May 1854. The law opened the two territories for settlement and proclaimed that the new residents would vote on whether slavery would be allowed in the territories. People on each

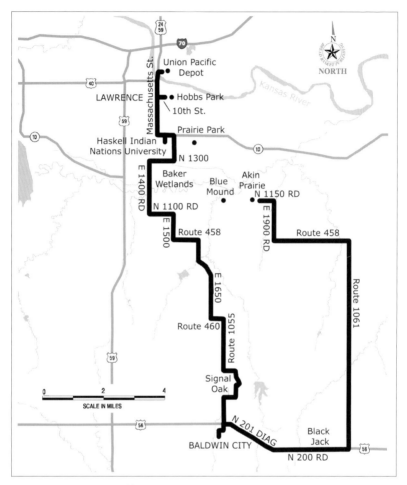

Tour 5: Lawrence to Baldwin

side of the slavery issue made a mad rush to get to Kansas and become residents. Pro-slavery Missourians—who already had 12,000 slaves living across the state line—got here first, of course, and began to stake claims along the eastern edge of Kansas and along the Kaw.

Within a month of the territory's opening, though, the New England Emigrant Aid Company sent Dr. Charles Robinson and Charles H. Brancomb with a small party of settlers to travel across the country and select a site for a town. Doctor Robinson had come through Kansas on his way to seek gold in California in 1849, and he remembered Mount Oread—now home to the University of Kansas—as a particularly beautiful spot. He and the first colonists arrived on the first of August 1854, and a second party from Massachusetts arrived about a month later. The town site was named Lawrence in honor of Amos A. Lawrence of Boston, a generous contributor to the New England Emigrant Aid Company.

Union Pacific Depot

Our first stop is the Union Pacific Depot at North Second and Locust streets, just across the Kansas River from Downtown Lawrence. The depot was completed in 1889 and served the railroad as a passenger depot until 1971. In 1984, the Union Pacific announced that it planned to tear down the building. Lawrence preservationists took action, and after a long struggle saved the building. As you enter the depot, you will notice that the depot is true to its historic character on the outside but modified considerably inside to serve as a visitor information center and meeting room.

Take the 30 minutes to see the movie presented inside, "Free State Fortress." It is a well-done film about the settling of Lawrence, seen through the eyes of a young couple who moved here from the East. Because it is a reenactment, the movie puts a human face on the historical facts and gives you a good context for understanding the historic sites you will see on this tour. Also pick up the brochure titled "Self-Guided Tour of Quantrill's Raid," which maps the sites involved in the Aug. 21, 1863, attack on Lawrence by William Quantrill and his band of guerillas.

The depot is a favorite with children, who are awed by the 100-some freight trains that speed by every day right outside the door. The depot is so well insulated that you can barely hear the trains from the inside, but you can go sit outside beside the tracks where kids often shriek with delight when the first locomotive roars past. (Don't worry, there's a tall fence between you and the trains.) Little ones also love to walk along the fence, looking for bits of coal that have fallen from the coal trains.

As you leave the depot, walk through the garden. It is a formal design inspired by French public gardens and a creation of the 1990s, but the limestone rocks used to make the raised beds are actually old curbstones. The sculpture in the center, "Mobility" by Shelly Bender, is one of many contemporary sculptures that you will see in Lawrence's parks and on Downtown sidewalks. At this writing, plans are under way to develop an area outside the Depot into a "Patriot's Memorial" honoring local residents who served in the military, the police force, or the Fire Department.

Kaw River levee

Walk south from the depot one block to the levee. You may see a big sign warning you of the health risk from eating fish caught here. The problem is chlordane, which concentrates in these fish, and eating more than one serving per month can put you past the recommended safe level of chlordane ingestion. (See the discussion of water quality issues in Chapter 2.) Nevertheless, you will see many people fishing here on a nice day.

Just below you is the Bowersock Dam, the only dam on the main stem of the Kaw. This spot has long been a favorite place for fishing, particularly for catfish. At the turn of the century, there was a thriving commercial fishing business here, and this side of the river was lined with little fishermen's shacks and boat rental shops. Fishermen used conventional nets and trap lines from flat-bottomed boats, but they also engaged in a risky business called "noodling." With a big hook tied to his wrist, a fisherman dived to the bottom of the dam and felt around in the darkness for the big catfish that lived there. He physically hooked the fish, and dragged it to the surface.

Back then, plenty of the fish were huge. Francis H. Snow, KU's chancellor at the turn of the century and presumably a reliable witness, wrote in 1875 that he saw a blue catfish weighing 175 pounds and heard of a 250-pounder. Commercial fishing was banned on the Kansas River in the 1920, but not on the Missouri, so some people continued to make a living as fishermen until all states along the Missouri banned catfish fishing in 1992.

Muddy water

Although water pollution is clearly the result of human occupation, it's not certain that the Kaw was ever a clear-running stream because of its geological history. The point where you are standing was close to the edge of a glacier that covered the central part of North America a million years ago. The huge sheet of ice passed over hills and valleys, bringing with it great loads of rock, gravel, sand, and clay that were ground and scraped from the surface of the land they traversed. Boulders of red quartzite and granite, dragged from Minnesota and South Dakota, can be found throughout eastern Kansas. (There's a red quartzite boulder at the south end of the bridge you will soon cross into Downtown Lawrence, but it was transported here from the Topeka area.) Glacial till, the particles left behind by the glaciers, created the deep, fertile soils of

Dam attracts industry, wildlife

The Bowersock Dam was built after decades of unsuccessful attempts at navigation by steamer. When Fort Riley to the west was established in 1853, the military sent several shipments up the river when the water was high, and many other steamboat operators arrived in hopes of trading upriver. The sternwheeler Lightfoot of Quindaro was specially designed for the Kansas River, but it spent more than a month in 1857 making the round trip from Kansas City to Lawrence, most of the time stuck on sandbars.

Giving up on river trade, the Legislature declared the Kaw non-navigable, and the Bowersocks built the dam in 1876 to provide power to the fledgling city. Lawrence was one of few cities in the West that had electricity in 1878, when Edison worked out the bugs in the incandescent light bulb and started the electric age. The Bowersock power plant attracted a number of industries to Lawrence.

Among those that thrived were four competing barbed wire companies, one of which occupied the building to the right of the Spring Hill Suites Hotel. (The building is now a

this region, and left the stream beds full of soft sediments. Even if there were no agriculture or urban development in the Kansas River Valley, the water might still be cloudy because of its soft bottom and banks.

The river at this location can be slow, shallow, and braided with sandbars in dry seasons. It can rage furiously in wet seasons. Throughout its history, Lawrence has suffered devastating floods. In the most recent flood year, 1993, the river reached the promenade of the hotel across the river. Lawrence dodged the bullet that year, when cities all over the Midwest were inundated despite all the reservoirs and levees that have been built in the past century to control flooding. In 1903 and 1951, though, the river flooded Lawrence, and many North Lawrence homes and businesses were lost.

restaurant complex called Abe and Jake's Landing, in honor of a couple of those early catfish fishermen.) The first barbed wire manufacturer started doing business here in 1878, shortly after barbed wire was invented, and Lawrence quickly became the barbed wire capital of the West because transportation costs were much lower than from Eastern manufacturing plants. The four competing companies eventually merged into one and were acquired by an East Coast company that moved the business out of Lawrence in 1898.

Other industries that located on the river in order to buy the power from Bowersock Dam included a paper mill, a flour mill, and a chemical manufacturer. Today, the Bowersock Dam still produces power that is sold to the local utility, Kansas Power and Light.

The dam also keeps the river free of ice during the winter, which attracts bald eagles to feed on fish, disabled waterfowl, and carrion. The eagles winter along the Kaw and on the reservoirs of its tributaries from mid-October to mid-March. As many as 30 bald eagles have been seen perched in the cottonwood trees on the north bank of the river just to your left.

The Douglas County Courthouse is one of several notable nineteenth-century buildings in Lawrence.

Downtown Lawrence

Return to your car and drive south across the bridge into Downtown Lawrence. Stay in the left lane, and turn left at the end of the bridge, then turn right onto Massachusetts Street. Downtown Lawrence is best seen from a walking tour, and if you've never done it, you should come back again when you have time to explore the downtown's wonderful old buildings, unique shops, and good dining. The National Trust for Historic Preservation recently released its first list of a Dozen Distinctive Destinations—12 American places to visit that are well-preserved and unique—and Lawrence was on the list.

The most important event in Lawrence's early history took place on this street, when William Quantrill and 450 men made a

The former Watkins Bank is now home to the Watkins Community Museum.

dawn attack on the city. The most important landmark is the Eldridge Hotel at the corner of Seventh and Massachusetts, which was burned down in 1861 during the Border Wars, rebuilt, and then burned again by Quantrill in 1863. Again it was rebuilt, and again it was damaged—this time in 1911 by a tornado. Since then, the building has undergone several transformations from hotel to apartments and back to a hotel. The brochure you picked up at the Depot has a map and description of other important sites from Quantrill's raid.

As you approach 11th Street, look for a parking space. On the corner of 11th and Massachusetts is the Watkins Community Museum of History, a three-story red brick building across from the limestone Douglas County Courthouse. Built in 1888 as a bank, the museum is worth a visit for its architecture as much as for its exhibits.

After you leave the museum, turn left (east) on 11th Street and and drive the few blocks to Delaware Street, where you will turn left at Hobbs Park. At 10th and Delaware is a restored stone house called the Murphy-Bromelsick House, for the Irish and German immigrants who lived in it after it was built in 1866. The house was recently saved from demolition by a community group and was moved from its original location nearby to this site, which was the farmstead of John Speer, an early resident of Lawrence. He came here from Pennsylvania in 1854 to support the abolitionist cause. Speer, the owner of a newspaper, was targeted by Quantrill's raiders because of his staunch opposition to slavery. He escaped the murderers, but two of his sons were killed.

This Hobbs Park Memorial is the beginning of what many civic leaders hope will become a series of historic sites to put Lawrence on the map of Civil War tourism. City leaders have their sights set on eventually having a museum devoted to the abolitionist movement.

Haskell University

Retrace your path back to Massachusetts Streets, and turn left, then turn left on 23rd Street. On your right is Haskell Indian Nations University, which has an average enrollment of 950 Native American students representing 152 Indigenous Nations from across the United States.

In 1882, Congress authorized the construction of three industrial training schools for Indian children, in Nebraska, Kansas, and Oklahoma, to assimilate Native American children into mainstream America. According to the Haskell University web site, "The United States wanted to solve the 'Indian problem' and they viewed education as the fastest and most complete means of achieving that end. It was felt that removing Indian children from their families and communities would remove the influences preventing the American Indian from becoming productive and acceptable members of the dominant society."

Congressman Dudley C. Haskell of Lawrence proposed his town as the site for the Kansas school and argued successfully that the availability of electricity in Lawrence made it the best choice. Haskell Institute opened its doors in 1884, and it had 280 children enrolled by January 1885. Today, Haskell has a 320-acre campus with 12 sites on the National Register of Historic Landmarks. You are welcome to walk around the campus to see the beautiful limestone buildings.

Haskell is in the process of building a cultural center and museum to house its archive collections, artifacts and oral histories projects. The visitor's center will be on the north end of campus.

Prairie Park

If you're traveling with restless children, a great place to stop next is Prairie Park Nature Center, a few blocks east of Haskell 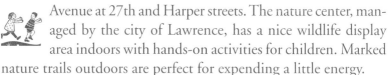 Avenue at 27th and Harper streets. The nature center, managed by the city of Lawrence, has a nice wildlife display area indoors with hands-on activities for children. Marked nature trails outdoors are perfect for expending a little energy.

Baker Wetlands

Turn south on Haskell Avenue, then west on 31st Street. On your left is the Baker Wetlands, a rare example of prairie wetlands, which once bordered rivers throughout this area but were generally drained and cleared for agriculture. Look for a driveway on your left, and pull in there, or park on the side of the road and walk in. Although there are no signs, you are welcome here; the land is owned by Baker University in Baldwin and is frequented by bird watchers and nature lovers.

This 573-acre tract in the floodplain of the Wakarusa River is teeming with life—home to more than 240 species of plant, 150 species of bird, including 40 that nest here, 30 different kinds of reptile and amphibian, and nearly 20 species of mammal. A boardwalk meanders through part of the wetlands, giving you an opportunity to see some of these plants and animals up close without getting your feet wet. There's also a trail along the perimeter of the tract.

Besides their role as critical habitat for many animals, wetlands serve other valuable functions. A wetland acts as a sponge during heavy rains, storing rainwater and reducing flood peaks. It also act as a filter, trapping sediment and using nutrients that otherwise would flow into the river. Yet their ecological importance has been ignored throughout most of the past 200 years. Kansas has lost more than half its wetlands in that time, destroyed by urbanization and by flood-control measures such as channelization, dams, and levees.

This remnant survives because it is poor farmland. The heavy clay soil and poor drainage made it undesirable to the early settlers, and so it hadn't been claimed by the time the federal government created the school that is now Haskell Indian Nations University.

Although most of the students at Haskell were not from agricultural tribes, the government decided to teach farming when the school opened and tried to drain and clear the land for that purpose. The agricultural effort was never successful, for natural and social reasons, and the wetlands were finally abandoned as a farm

The Baker Wetlands is teeming with life, and visitors can view the plant and animal species up close.

The boardwalk at the Baker Wetlands allows easy—and dry—access to wildlife.

in the 1950s. The government leased and then eventually deeded the land to Baker University for use as an ecological reserve and research site.

The wetlands have been at the center of a development controversy in Lawrence for more than a decade. Government officials want to build a highway around the city and have completed the first leg on the west side of Lawrence. But the route on the eastern side of the city eventually was scuttled because of potential harm to the wetlands and to a religious ceremonial site on the Haskell University campus. At this writing, alternative sites nearby are being considered, but no decisions have been reached.

Wakarusa River floodplain

Leaving the wetlands, continue west to Louisiana Street, then turn south. On your right is a field that is more representative of most eastern Kansas floodplains—drained, monocropped, and lacking in biological diversity.

As you look across this wide floodplain, you might expect that you're coming to a big river, but you will be disappointed when you reach the bridge. The Wakarusa River is quite modest by river standards. Geologists suggest that the disproportionately large floodplain may be the result of glaciation, which blocked the flow of water down the Kaw River and forced it into the Wakarusa. This made the Wakarusa into a major river — possibly as big as the Mississippi—for a time and caused extensive erosion of the land around it. When the glaciers receded and water began to flow down the Kaw, the Wakarusa became the narrow stream with steep banks that you see today. The condition is what is known as a "misfit stream."

Even small rivers such as this one presented problems for travelers in covered wagons. Beginning in the late 1830 and continuing through the 1850s, thousands of ordinary families passed through here on the Oregon Trail; this location was one of several places where they crossed the Wakarusa River. In 1854, a bridge called Blanton's Bridge was built at this spot, so most travelers after that time passed across the river right where you are. As you continue south, notice the old house on your right, where a sign claims it was homesteaded in 1854.

Blue Mound and the disappearance of prairie

At the stop sign, North 1100 Road, turn left. You will be following the route of the Oregon Trail, though going in the wrong direction. The Oregon Trail was used almost entirely by people moving west, and few came back this way after surviving the 2,000-mile journey to the West Coast. The Santa Fe Trail, in contrast, was used primarily by traders going back and forth to the Southwest.

At the next stop sign, look straight ahead, and you will see Blue Mound slightly to the north of the road. Besides being a landmark for travelers in the 1800s, it served briefly as a ski slope in the 1970s, when it was called Mont Bleu and covered with artificially manufactured snow. Geologically, Blue Mound is known as a monadnock, an island-like hill that remained after the surrounding terrain eroded. Its limestone cap, like those of other hills around Lawrence, prevented Blue Mound from eroding.

Vinland Valley

Turn right on East 1500 Road, and follow the signs for Douglas County Route 1055. As you reach the intersection with Route 460, you will be in the beautiful Vinland Valley. Ahead of you is the Vinland Valley Aerodrome, a grass strip used mostly by small planes and crop dusters. Go straight ahead to the tiny settlement of Vinland, which has the first library in the state and several other old buildings.

Forestation of the prairie

Blue Mound and other hills in this area were devoid of trees when Lawrence was settled. Maps and photographs of the period show trees along the rivers and streams, but otherwise the landscape was open prairie, a fact commented on repeatedly by early settlers. A survey of land in the 1850s showed that 93% of Douglas County was tallgrass prairie. Once settlers started moving here, the prairie quickly began to disappear, replaced by woodlands of thorny trees.

Several factors caused this quick transformation from tallgrass prairie to the thick woods cloaking the hills before you today. The most important factor was fire. Before settlement, fires regularly swept the prairie, preventing trees from becoming established. In some cases, lightning was to blame, but ecologists now think that native peoples also may have set fires, both accidentally and as a management tool. In any case, once the Indians were relocated to Oklahoma, and white settlers built houses, prairie fires became much less frequent.

Grazing by massive herds of bison and elk also kept trees off the prairie, but those animals were hunted to near-extinction. The cattle that were brought to graze the land were much pickier about what they ate, shunning the prickly cedar and thorny locusts that began to invade the prairie.

A third factor in the disappearance of the prairie was the settlers' practice of planting trees in abundance. Before white settlers arrived, there just weren't many tree seeds around to germinate on the prairie. The settlers planted trees in town because they missed the shady landscapes of their homes in the East, and they did it in the country to provide firewood, fencing and windbreaks for their farms. In fact, in 1867 the Legislature agreed to subsidize the planting of hedgerows, at the rate of $128 per mile because of the fear that the native timber would soon be used up.

As you travel south on this tour, you will notice many fields are surrounded by hedgerows. The tree of choice was Osage Orange because its wood is hard and virtually indestructible. When burned, it makes an extremely hot fire. The Osage Orange tree came to be known as "hedge," and many of the knobby fence posts you see strung with barbed wire throughout the countryside are hedge posts.

In a study of fence posts at Oregon State University, Osage Orange posts were found to be 100% intact, with no signs of decay, after 66 years. The hedge posts were far more durable than any other untreated wood, and even more durable than steel posts. Osage Orange, *Maclura pomifera*, is easily recognizable from mid-summer on by its grapefruit-sized green fruits, known as "hedge apples."

The state subsidy for hedgerow planting expired in the 1870s when barbed wire arrived in Kansas, but the tradition of planting hedges around fields continued for many more years because hedges sheltered farms from the incessant prairie wind. In the past few decades, many hedgerows have been torn out because farm equipment has gotten too massive to maneuver around them. Some farmers also have viewed the hedgerow as wasted land that could be used for crops; the U.S. Department of Agriculture estimates that 2 acres are taken out of production for every mile of hedgerow. More recent research, however, shows that wind reduces crop growth and yield, and farmers are not gaining when they remove their hedges.

Although it may seem that there's not much left of Vinland, it is a viable community. People are dispersed on farms throughout the valley, but they have strong social ties. There's an elementary school, now part of the Baldwin School District, and a Methodist church. And on the third weekend in August every year, Vinland puts on a country fair straight out of a Norman Rockwell painting. Held at the pretty fairgrounds on the north side of the road, the Vinland Fair features good country cooking, a homemade ice cream contest (with samples for 25 cents), a pet parade for children, a talent show, and much more—all very low-tech, neighborly, and nostalgic.

Baldwin Woods

Leaving Vinland, return to Route 1055 and head south again. The road gets hillier, the forest alongside it more dense. Turn left on North 500 Road, and slow down to take in the cool, moist darkness of the forest known as Baldwin Woods. This is a rare treasure for Kansas: designated a National Natural Landmark in 1980, it is described as "a unique remnant oak-hickory stand approaching climax condition, located at the western edge of the eastern deciduous forest."

Although hardwood forests can be found elsewhere in Kansas, the diversity of species declines the farther west you go. These woods, for example, are the limit of the range for white oaks. The Baldwin Woods are native to this area, not the result of prairie destruction as was the case with the hillsides farther north. These woods exist because of the unusually steep north-facing slope with several creeks that keep the land cool and moist.

This tract survived the destruction of the settlement years because the people of Baldwin decided that the woods should be maintained as a place to provide much-needed timber. Rather than clear-cutting the hillside, as happened with many oak groves along the Kansas River, the Baldwin residents cut selectively and kept the forest healthy. The 200-acre tract is now owned by the University of Kansas and treated as a biological reserve. The land is not open to the public.

Although the Signal Oak is gone, the beautiful vista from its hilltop home remains.

Signal Oak

Go south on East 1750 Road, and you will climb that steep north slope. Once you reach the top of the hill, watch on your right for a sign for Signal Oak. Here, during the Bleeding Kansas days, stood a majestic white oak tree that reportedly was used for hanging lanterns to warn people on Mount Oread that raiders were in the area. From this magnificent vantage point, you can easily spot Mount Oread by looking for the red roofs of the University of Kansas. The tree itself, which died, is now gone.

At this point, you are leaving the watershed of the Kansas River; from here south, streams flow to the Marais des Cygne River.

Baldwin and Baker University

Take Eighth Street into the center of Baldwin. On your left is Baker University, the state's first college, founded in 1858. Park on Eighth Street, and walk onto the beautiful campus, across a stone bridge over a cascading stream, to the stone chapel ahead of you. The chapel once resided in the small English town of Sproxton, but when the congregation there disbanded, the church sat empty for seven years. Baker University officials bought the chapel, had it disassembled stone by stone, and shipped to Baldwin, where it was rebuilt and renamed the Clarice L. Osborne Memorial Chapel. A service is held at 11 a.m. every Thursday during the academic year, and the chapel is open all day for quiet reflection and prayer.

On the other side of the chapel is the Collins Sports Center; directly behind it, on Fifth Street, is a museum known as the Old Castle Museum, though in fact located in a rustic and simple building, the first one erected for the college.

Baldwin is a pleasant, shady town, proud of its sugar maple trees that turn bright red in fall, and its streets of Victorian architecture.

East of town, on High Street, is the Midland Railway Depot, a landmark on the National Register of Historic Places. From late May until late October, you can take a one-hour train ride on the Midland Railway. The railway is a volunteer-staffed demonstration railroad that runs 12-mile excursions on a line originally constructed in 1867. The early 1900s train travels through woods and fields to Norwood, a long-abandoned town, and back to the station. It's a particular treat for young children who have never ridden a train before.

The Santa Fe Trail and Black Jack

When you leave Baldwin, go east on U.S. 56, and you will be traveling the route of the Santa Fe Trail. This time, you won't be going the wrong direction because the Santa Fe Trail was used primarily by traders who moved back and forth between Kansas City and the Mexican border. The Santa Fe Trail was widely used from 1825, when it was surveyed by the government, until railroads made it obsolete in the 1870s.

Three miles east of town is a memorial to the Battle of Black Jack, which featured the noted abolitionist John Brown. He operated in Kansas for several years before he attacked the federal arsenal at Harper's Ferry, West Virginia. Brown was angry about the Sack of Lawrence on May 21, 1856, in which the pro-slavery sher-

This cabin marks the site of the Battle of Black Jack, where abolitionist John Brown killed five men and fought off a deputy U.S. marshal.

iff and his posse burned down the Free State Hotel and threw the newspaper's presses into the river. Brown killed five pro-slavery men and then was confronted at Black Jack by Captain Henry C. Pate, deputy U.S. marshal. Brown and his band fought off Pate's party, but the event unleashed battles between free state and pro-slavery antagonists all along the state border.

The memorial to the battle is on the edge of another Baker University natural area, a virgin prairie where wagon ruts from the Santa Fe Trail are clearly visible.

Conservation easements

Leaving Black Jack, continue east on U.S. 56 for about one mile, then turn left (north) on Douglas County Route 1061. Go north 8 miles, then west on Douglas County Route 458 for almost 3 miles, then turn north on East 1900 Road (Route 1057). Go about one mile to North 1150 Road, and turn west. About half a mile later, on your left, you will see a sign for the Akin Prairie.

This piece of native prairie has been preserved by a conservation easement to the Kansas Land Trust. KLT is a non-profit organization based in Lawrence that protects and preserves land of ecological, scenic, agricultural, historic, and recreational significance.

Formed in 1990 in response to the destruction of another native prairie west of Lawrence, KLT went to the Legislature and got a statute that allows landowners to voluntarily place conservation easements on their land.

Most other states have similar laws, and conservation easements have become a powerful tool for preserving land. A conservation easement is a legally binding agreement, designed by the landowner, to control the type or amount of use on the property in the future. In return, the landowner receives tax benefits. Congress has been particularly generous in providing tax breaks for easements in and near urban areas.

This particular piece of land is 17 acres of high-quality prairie (that is, it harbors a high number of species) that has never been plowed. It is colorful with wildflowers in summer and lush with tall grasses. The easement on it was donated in 1994 by Tom O. Akin in memory of his late wife, Dorothy, who loved this spot more than any other on their farm. Because of Mr. Akin's dedication to this land, it will remain a little piece of wild Kansas forever.

For more information

- ✓ Lawrence Visitor Information Center, 402 N. 2nd St., Lawrence, KS 66044; 785-865-4499; cvb@visitlawrence.com; www.visitlawrence.com.
- ✓ Prairie Park Nature Center, 3730 Harper, Lawrence, KS 66046; 785-832-7980.
- ✓ Midland Railway, P.O. Box 412, Baldwin City, KS 66006; 800-651-0388; www.midland-ry.org/midland.html.
- ✓ Kansas Land Trust, P.O. Box 116, Lawrence, KS 66046; 785-749-3297.

Lawrence to Lecompton to Clinton Lake

This tour contains some important "Bleeding Kansas" historic sites, but its primary focus is on ecological features of the watershed. It begins at the edge of Downtown Lawrence and travels west to Lecompton on the Scenic River Road, which is gravel for several miles. Then the tour circles Clinton Lake, all on paved road. This tour is primarily a driving and museum trip, but you will have the opportunity to do some hiking and bird watching, so wear comfortable shoes and bring your binoculars.

Go west on 6th Street to Indiana and turn north (right). The names of the early north-south streets in Lawrence progress in the order in which states were admitted to the Union. The naming of the streets began with Delaware on the east side, which allowed the main street to be called Massachusetts in honor of the first settlers' home state.

Water treatment

At the corner of 2nd and Indiana streets is the Lawrence water treatment plant, and just beyond it is Burcham Park, where water is drawn from the Kansas River. The Kaw provides about 45% of the city's water supply, with the rest coming from Clinton Reservoir, which is on the Wakarusa River. Most cities, towns, and rural water districts in the Kansas River Valley rely on the river for their water supplies.

The importance of the Kaw for residential, industrial, and agricultural use cannot be overemphasized. More than 40% of the

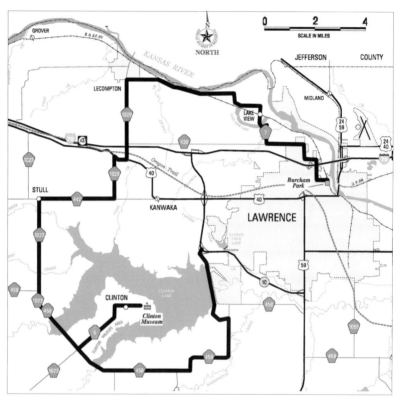

Tour 6: Lawrence to Clinton via Lecompton.

state's population now lives in the 10 counties that border the Kaw, and this area is the fastest growing in the state. As a result, the water quality in the Kansas River is a subject of concern for everyone interested in quality of life in the valley.

At this writing, the Kaw frequently fails to meet federal clean water standards. Sources of pollution in the Kaw include sewage treatment plants from cities upstream, livestock operations, failing septic tanks, and farm fields. Some efforts outlined in the state plan for cleaning up the Kaw include tougher enforcement of septic tank codes, improving livestock waste management, and restoring natural marsh and wooded areas along the river banks. (For more information on water quality, see Chapter 2.)

Riverfront parks

These wooded areas along streams are known as riparian zones, and you will get a chance to walk through one in Burcham Park. Restoring natural areas along the rivers is compatible with recreation, and Lawrence was one of the first cities on the Kaw to develop recreational sites along its waterfront.

A riparian zone is that small border where land and river meet and often merge. It is a complex ecosystem rich in biodiversity, where many kinds of animals and plants feed and live. The movement of the river, rising and falling with the seasons and storms, creates habitats that exist nowhere else and are critical to the survival of many species. (See Plants of the Riparian Zone on the next page.)

Besides their value to wildlife, riparian zones are important because they act as filters, removing contaminants from water that runs off the land into the river. Agricultural chemicals, oil and gas from roads, litter, sediment, and other pollutants are trapped in the riparian zone and, through complex mechanisms not well understood, are cleaned up by the plants. This process makes the restoration of riparian areas an important first step in any effort to improve the water quality in the river. Land that was once cleared right up to the riverbanks for industry or farming is, in some places, being replanted in native trees, shrubs, and grasses. As you stroll along the river bank, take an admiring look at these amazing plants.

Leave Burcham Park and go right to Michigan. Follow Michigan north to the bend in the road, which will take you to the Scenic River Road. At the intersection of Route 438 and Route 7, where you turn north, you will see the homestead of Eben Baldwin, a prosperous farmer, county commissioner, and part owner of a Lawrence brick factory in the late 1800s. (The property is not open to the public.) The barn, one of the most ambitious ever built in this area, was made of native limestone in 1879 and has never been significantly altered. The rafters are hand hewn, and everything is joined with wood spikes.

The homestead was locally famous for the ingenious system that brought indoor plumbing to the house earlier than at most farms. Rainwater from the huge roof was collected in a cistern beside the barn. A windmill pumped the water into the attic of the

Plants of the riparian zone

One of the most imposing plants along the riparian zone is the Eastern cottonwood tree, *Populus deltoides*, the state tree of Kansas. The cottonwood is a fast-growing tree that reaches nearly 100 feet high along stream banks and half that height elsewhere. It has gray bark and flat, triangular leaves that rustle in even the slightest breeze. In early summer, the female trees drop their seeds, which are carried in the air by tufts of "cottony" hairs that give the tree its common name. You may have seen "cottonless" cottonwoods for sale at local nurseries; those are male plants that don't make seeds.

Cottonwoods have soft wood and rarely live past 70 years old, because storms destroy their huge limbs. Cottonwoods were important to the settlement of the state because most of Kansas was covered with prairie when Europeans arrived here. The only wood for building was in the riparian areas.

Another big presence on the banks of the Kaw is sycamore trees, easily identified by their patchy white bark and their fruits, small brown balls that dangle on the trees into winter. Other big trees commonly found in the riparian zone are green ash and American elm. The woods in this particular area have been harvested periodically, particularly when Lawrence was first settled.

The smaller trees along the river are less impressive but just as important in the riparian ecosystem. Willows, for example, make low, dense thickets that provide protective cover for birds and other wildlife; some songbirds use the silky seeds of willows to line their nests. Willows also have extensive root systems that help prevent erosion of the banks.

farmhouse, where it was stored in a copper lined tank. Gravity provided water to the indoor plumbing.

Lakeview

As the road curves through the river bottom here, you will

come to a sign for the Lakeview Club on the edge of a small lake. This lake is a natural feature called an oxbow lake, created when the flooding river cut a new channel and left behind a U-shaped loop of river where the channel formerly ran. The term "oxbow" is a vestige of our agricultural heritage, when everyone was familiar with the yokes used to hook oxen together for farm work and travel. The oxbow was the U-shaped piece that ran beneath the oxen's heads.

Oxbow lakes are fairly common along rivers, and they reflect the fact that a river meanders across its floodplain. Water moves through the river channel at different velocities. As it approaches a bend, water on the outside of the bend moves faster than water on the inside of the bend and cuts into the bank, thus eroding it. On on the inside of the bend, the slower-moving water drops sediment, thus building up that shore. With this constant erosion and deposition, the river slowly changes its course over time, but when water is rushing through the channel during floods, those changes can occur quickly.

It is not known exactly when the Kaw changed its course here and left this oxbow lake, but Lakeview was here when Lawrence was founded in the 1850s. Although most oxbow lakes drain or dry up within a few decades, Lakeview Lake has persisted, in part because the railroad embankment dams up the ends of the lake, and in part because members of the Lakeview Club have dredged the lake periodically.

Lakeview was once a highly desirable club, back in the days when local residents didn't have other lakes or swimming pools to go to for summer recreation. Although it has lost some of its luster, it is still cherished by the people who hold memberships there and have built cabins along its shores. It is not open to the public, but you can catch a glimpse from the road.

Through the floodplain

The road continues to wind along, essentially moving back toward the river, which has looped to the north at this location. You're now in the floodplain, and as you look across these broad,

The Kaw deposits sediment that forms sandbars, which support river biodiversity.

On the sandbar

Sandbars develop when the river picks up a big load of sediment during high flow and then drops the sediment downstream where the river widens and slows down. As the water flow decreases, the heavier particles fall out first, followed by gradually smaller particles, so the sediment is sorted with rocks and gravel on the bottom and sand or silt on top. Sandbars continually shift, though less so than they did when water flow was not controlled by upstream dams.

Sandbars, along with other obstructions like mud flats and gravel bars, are a critical part of the river ecosystem because they create shallow areas where wildlife can feed, nest, and rest. According to the Kansas Biological Survey, these shallow areas support three-fourths of the life in the river, with only one-fourth living in the deep water or open channel.

At least 100 species of aquatic and semi-aquatic invertebrates, and dozens of species of birds, mammals, reptiles, amphibians, and fish depend on these shallow areas of the river. Wading birds like herons and egrets are often seen in the shallows along the sandbars, feeding on the fish that are themselves there feeding and breeding, away from the fast water.

flat fields, it's easy to imagine the river washing out over them during periods of flooding.

Flooding is a natural part of a river ecosystem; in fact, the deposition of sediments by flooding is the reason that this is such fertile farmland. But for most of this century, government policy has been to try to control flooding with dams, levees, channels, and other engineering projects. Although there are no reservoirs on the main stem of the Kaw, 18 reservoirs exist on the smaller rivers that flow into the Kaw. About 85% of the drainage area of this river is controlled by dams. Today, floods are far less common than fifty years ago, but these fields still flood easily.

On this road, you haven't been able to get a good look at the river yet, because it is shielded from view by the riparian area. Soon the road will rise along the base of a steep hillside. When it does, you have come up from the floor of the Kansas River valley, which is bordered on both sides along its entire length by bluffs ranging from 25 feet to 400 feet above the valley floor. Suddenly, the air is cooler, and in winter the road will have ice on it long after it has melted below. The woods on this hillside are typical of upland woodlands along the river. Several kinds of oaks and hickory and other hardwoods predominate.

At a few places on the road, you will get some excellent views of the river. If the river is low, you will see a mosaic of sandbars dotting the channel.

Lecompton

When the river road ends, turn right to go into Lecompton. This town of 800 people played an important role in the settlement of Kansas and the struggle over slavery. Lecompton was established in 1854 and named Bald Eagle, probably because of the huge numbers of eagles that wintered on the banks of the Kaw just north of town. (You can still see a few here in winter.) The name was soon changed in honor of a federal judge, S.D. Lecompte.

The proslavery legislature that took power in Kansas after fraudulent elections—in which thousands of Missourians voted illegally—chose Lecompton as the territorial capital in 1855. For a

A pro-slavery constitution was written in Constitution Hall in Lecompton.

few years, Lecompton thrived: Its population reached 4,000, it boasted five fine hotels, stage and ferry served it, and it became known as "Wall Street of the West" because the settlers and land speculators poured into the federal land office to stake their claims.

You can visit that land office in Constitution Hall, now managed as a state historic site. The plain white building was erected in 1855, after the Free State party drafted a state constitution at Topeka. When the U.S. Congress did not recognize that first constitution, the Territorial Capital was officially moved to Lecompton. In 1857, the proslavery Territorial Legislature meeting at Lecompton wrote the Lecompton Constitution, which called for Kansas to enter the union as a slave state.

While this new Kansas constitution was being debated by Congress—an incendiary debate that started the nation down the path to Civil War—a third constitution was drafted at Leavenworth and approved by the people of Kansas in 1858. That constitution also failed to win acceptance in Washington. Finally, a constitutional convention met in July 1859 in Wyandot, now part of Kansas City, Kansas, and was adopted by popular vote in October 1859.

The Wyandot constitution declared that Kansas would be a free state. The U.S. House of Representatives voted in April 1860 to accept the constitution and admit Kansas to the union. The proslavery majority in the U.S. Senate, however, refused to act on the Kansas constitution. The Republican candidate for president, Abraham Lincoln, ran on a platform of immediate admission to the union for Kansas. When Lincoln won the election, Southern states seceded from the nation and removed their representatives from Congress. Both houses of Congress then passed the bill admitting Kansas to the nation, and President James Buchanan signed the bill into law on Jan. 29, 1861. Kansas, after much turmoil, that day became the 34th state of a rapidly disintegrating nation.

But back to Lecompton in 1855, at the start of all those troubles: Congress appropriated $50,000 for construction of a capitol building, and Italian stonemason Mark Migliario was summoned from St. Louis to build it. But as free state forces took power in Kansas and the capital was moved to Topeka, the incomplete Lecompton capitol was abandoned. The building was taken over by the United Brethren Church in Christ, completed in 1882, and opened as Lane University. The square stone building is now a museum. Be sure to see the ornate chapel on the second floor.

Down along the river bluffs at the end of Second Street is a small park with a stone building also built by Mark Migliario as a ferry house. It served as headquarters of the Democratic Party headquarters during the Territorial period.

Oregon Trail and Stull

Go south from Lecompton on Route 1029, then go west on U.S. 40 for about a mile; the Oregon Trail followed this ridge dividing the Wakarusa and Kansas river watersheds. For a few minutes, you will be able to enjoy the splendid view in both directions. Myra Eels, who traveled the Oregon Trail in 1838, made this comment in her journal as she passed through this area: "Scenery delightful. Meet Indians at every encampment."

Turn south again on Route 1029. When you reach N. 1600 Road, go right into the town of Stull. This village was settled by

German immigrants in the 1860s, and church services were said in German until after the turn of the century. Many people living here are descendants of those early settlers. On your right is the Stull Cemetery. Until 1999, a huge pine tree stood in front of the adjacent ruins of the German Evangelical Church, built in 1867 and razed in 2002. The combination of tombstones, sheltering tree, and ruined church created a memorable landmark that was the subject of many photographs. The tree succumbed in 1999 to pine wilt, a disease that is ravaging several species of pine trees in eastern Kansas.

You will turn left on Route 1023 at the Methodist Church in Stull, and as you travel south, you're likely to see many windbreaks and ornamental plantings of pine trees that are infected. Pine wilt is caused by the pinewood nematode, which blocks the flow of resin within the tree and causes the needles to turn brown and remain on the tree. A tree usually dies within three months of infection. The nematode is carried by a wood-boring beetle called the pine sawyer, which emerges from infected trees in May and flies to new trees, which then become infected. There is no cure for pine wilt; the only hope is to prevent its spread by cutting down and burning infected trees before the beetles emerge around May 1.

Around Clinton Lake

Leaving Stull, you will cross Deer Creek, one of three tributaries to Clinton Lake. Rising above the south bank of Deer Creek is an area of upland woodlands. These densely covered hillsides often open up into native prairies on the hilltops. And the woods tend to be found on the north sides of these hills. Biologists assume this patterns occurs because wildfires, fanned by the prevailing southerly winds, kept the south sides of the hills cleared of trees, but died out before they burned down the north slopes.

The road you're traveling borders Clinton Lake, which was built by the U.S. Army Corps of Engineers beginning in 1971 for flood control and water supply. The gates on the dam were closed in 1977, and the lake gradually filled over the next three years. The road crosses the spot where the Wakarusa River enters the reservoir, and you should pull off to the shoulder to get your first clear view of the lake and to do some bird watching.

When the lake was built, trees were removed from the main part of the lake but left in the arms to provide habitat for fish. Now, more than 20 years later, most of the trees have rotted, but you will still see some snags standing above the water. These shal-

Watching the water

Deciding how much water to keep in those reservoirs is a complicated business. Each lake is supposed to keep a certain level, known as the multipurpose pool, to provide water supply and recreation. But above that level, the Corps can play around a bit to achieve certain goals.

For example, lowering the lake to the multipurpose pool level leaves the shores of the lake exposed and allows vegetation to grow, which provides better fish habitat when the level rises in spring, which pleases the many people who fish on the lake. The level will be dropped again in summer, then brought up in fall to fill the areas in the upper arms of the lake to provide habitat for waterfowl, which pleases hunters. Some water is always flowing under the dam through a drainage pipe to preserve fisheries in the outlet area below the dam.

Clinton controls 70% of the Wakarusa River watershed, so one good thunderstorm can raise the lake level significantly, and the Corps can decide, based on what is happening downstream, whether to impound the water or let it go. In more than two decades of use, Clinton has risen only halfway to flood level. Should it ever reach its flood level, water would start to pour across the road at the north end of the dam and into the emergency spillway that runs parallel to the outlet. The spillway holds a paved path that is a great place to take kids for biking and roller skating without having to worry about cars.

lows provide food and rest for millions of migrating birds each spring and fall. You may see huge numbers of white pelicans here seasonally and great blue herons year-round. Painted buntings, one of the most colorful birds in North America, have been spotted here in the past few years, although this is north of their traditional range.

Although the shallow areas of the lake are good for wildlife,

Bald eagles' fortunes

The bald eagle is one of the greatest success stories of the Endangered Species Act of 1973. In 1963, only 417 breeding pairs remained in the lower 48 states, down from an estimated half-million individual birds when Congress chose the eagle as our national symbol in 1782.

Bald eagles began to decline by the 1900s because of habitat loss, a decline in food, and killing by people who considered them competitors for fish. In 1940, Congress passed the Bald Eagle Protection Act, which made it illegal to kill, harm, harass, or possess bald eagles, alive or dead, and the restrictions also applied to eggs, feathers, and nests.

For a time, the eagles began to recover, but then came DDT, a pesticide used to control mosquitoes. DDT caused eagles to lay thin-shelled eggs that often broke during incubation. DDT was banned from use in the United States in 1972, and, shortly thereafter, the bald eagle was listed as an endangered or threatened species throughout the lower 48 states.

Federal and state agencies worked together to improve conditions for the eagles, and slowly but steadily their numbers recovered. Today, the bald eagle numbers 5,800 breeding pairs, and is nearing recovery. The bald eagle's status was reduced from endangered to threatened in 1995, and the bird is expected to be removed from the endangered species list in the near future.

they are creating an ever-increasing problem for Lawrence's water treatment plant, which gets more than half the city's water supply here. Rivers and creeks flowing into the lake carry nutrients, both natural and from agricultural and municipal runoff. The nutrients cause blooms of algae in the shallow parts of the lake. When the algae die, they give off a bad-tasting substance that gets into the water supply. The problem is not a health hazard, but it is one that will increase as the lakes age, fill with sediment, and have ever more shallow areas where the algae can grow.

The area on the right side of the road is interesting to observe over the course of the year. Sometimes it is covered with water, and thousands of birds will rest here. But when the lake water level is down, it is a big mud flat surrounded by dense stands of willows. The mud comes from the Wakarusa River, which drops its sediment as the water slows down upon entering the lake.

Bald eagle nest

Shortly after crossing the arm of the lake, turn left on Route 6, and follow the signs toward the town of Clinton. At the first bend in the road, turn right into the Clinton Wildlife Area, drive to the end of the road, and park. A short trail will take you to the edge of the lake, and from here you can get a good view of what has been one of the most productive bald eagle nests in the United States.

Kansas has become home to at least 14 breeding pairs that have successfully fledged more than 123 eaglets in the past decade. The first of those pairs built a nest in this arm of the lake in 1989. Despite the fact that the female disappeared during incubation and the male raised the birds alone, two eaglets were fledged that year. One of them returned to Kansas in 1993 and nested at Hillsdale Lake in Miami County, and the other returned in 1994 and nested at Perry Lake in Jefferson County.

Every year, a pair of eagles has come back to this area and successfully raised young—usually three eaglets, which is more than the national average. That first nest rotted and fell into the lake in

The banded leg of a bald eagle is about the same size as a woman's hand.

1998, but the pair rebuilt in the same tree the next year. From 1989 to 2001, this nest produced 33 eagles.

A second pair built a nest on the Wakarusa arm of the lake in 2000, and they have hatched and fledged four young the past two years. The male on that second nest was fledged from a nest at Wolf Creek in 1996, and the female came from the Chippewa National Forest in Minnesota. Eagles generally nest within 100 miles of where the male was fledged.

You are likely to see eagles in this area from early November to mid-July. The eagle lays eggs—about the size of a big chicken egg—between late January and March. The male and female sit

Michael A. Watkins of the U.S. Army Corps of Engineers cradles a juvenile bald eagle at Clinton Lake.

on them for a little over a month, until they hatch. Then the adults care for the young for 70 to 80 days before the offspring learn to fly.

By then, the eaglets have reached 95% of their adult size, and that 6-foot nest, which seemed huge when there were three chicken-sized eggs in it, will seem a little cramped with five birds that stand 3 feet tall from head to tail and that have wing-spans of 7 feet.

The young eagles will roost at the nest tree for about a month after fledging. The pair that nests on the Wakarusa arm and their young usually leave the lake in summer, presumably to find cooler weather in the north or west. But some of the other nesting pairs in the state do stay year-round.

The comings and goings of the Clinton eagles are fairly well documented because the U.S. Fish and Wildlife Service bands the birds and has even put radio transmitters on some of them. How do they manage to put a leg band on a bird as big and ferocious as a bald eagle? The preferred method is to do it when the birds are 6 weeks old, about 8 to 10 pounds.

After the parents have flown off the nest, a boat pulls up to the tree, and a tree climber scales up to the nest. Each bird is put in a gunny sack and lowered to the biologists waiting below. Even at that age, the eaglets are a handful, but the biologists attach leg bands, measure and photograph the birds, and return them to the nest in about 30 minutes. Contrary to popular belief, the parents will not abandon the baby birds if they smell humans on them. Eagles, like most birds, don't have much in the way of olfactory sense.

Adult birds can also be banded, and that's when this quiet arm of the lake gets really exciting. The scientists tether a decoy eagle near the shoreline, anchor a fish in place, and bury traps in the silt around the bait. When the adult eagle comes to feed, the traps catch it by a leg. The eagle is then hooded, which calms it down, and two bands are attached to its legs. One band is purple and white, which allows biologists to identify it from a distance as a Kansas eagle. Once the bands are attached, the biologists pull off the hood and release the bird.

Town of Clinton

Return to the paved road, turn right, and continue into the town of Clinton, which was known as Bloomington in 1855 when the first white settlers came to this rich valley between the Wakarusa River and Rock Creek. For some reason lost in history, a second settlement sprang up about a half-mile to the east and also took the name Bloomington. The first Bloomington changed its name to Winchester and later to Clinton.

The area was settled mostly by people opposed to slavery, so it was often targeted by border ruffians and proslavery forces. Several houses here were on the Underground Railroad, a series of places where escaped slaves could take refuge while passing through on their long journeys north to freedom.

In the summer, park rangers give programs outside the old Bloomington Smokehouse.

Proceed into the Corps' Bloomington Park area, where you will find the Clinton Museum, with exhibits about Clinton and towns that are now under water.

Clinton Dam

Return to Route 1023/458, and continue east into the beautiful and fertile Washington Creek valley, mercifully still used for farming unlike the hillsides that surround it. Just past Wakarusa Valley Elementary School, turn left at the sign for Clinton Lake. This road will carry you across the 1.75-mile dam, which is small compared to most Corps of Engineers projects.

On your right as you begin to cross the dam, you will see a golf course and, beyond it, a marshy area. The original channel of the Wakarusa River ran along the tree line there, and this area was a mosaic of wetlands.

After Clinton Dam was built, the land was used for farming, but in 1999, the city of Lawrence decided to return it to a wet meadow, which is an area primarily of grasses. Days after the bulldozers finished changing the contours of the field to stop the water from draining, flocks of ducks and geese began to visit the site.

Volunteers, including many schoolchildren, collected seeds from other wetlands and sowed them here. Reestablishment of wetlands is a slow process, and it will be many years before it begins to look like a natural wetland. A quarter-mile walking trail leads into the wetland (the path is built up so you won't get wet feet). If you'd like to stop, you can reach it by turning right at the end of the dam and following the access road that parallels the dam.

At the center of the dam is the tower housing the gate mechanism that controls the flow of water out of the lake. Two steel gates, operated hydraulically, cover a 13-foot-wide concrete conduit that runs below the dam. The gates are opened or closed on orders of the Kansas City office of the Corps of Engineers, which supervises all the dams on the Kansas River.

Continue north after you have crossed the dam to the Corps of Engineers visitor center. The center has a small exhibit about the floods that prompted Congress to authorize this dam. You can take an easy hike down to lookout point, the grassy hill that sticks out into the lake. There's also the state park, which charges admission, and offers camping, bicycling paths, boating and swimming.

For more information

➤ Constitution Hall and Territorial Capitol Museum (Lane University), Lecompton, KS; 785-887-6285; www.LecomptonKansas.com.

➤ Clinton Lake, U.S. Army Corps of Engineers office, 872 N. 1402 Rd., Lawrence, KS 66049; 785-843-7665.

Jefferson County

This tour focuses on the great outdoors—the plants, animals, and geology of hilly, rural Jefferson County. You will be taking several hikes to get close to nature, so choose a beautiful day, and wear appropriate clothes. It is necessary to drive on gravel roads for long portions of the tour.

The tour will begin at the Kansas Ecological Reserves, which straddle the border between Douglas and Jefferson counties. Take U.S. 24 & 40 east past the Lawrence Municipal Airport, and turn left (north) on E. 1600 Road. Follow 1600 as it curves around a few streams and hills, until you see the sign for the Ecological Reserves. A short distance beyond the sign, on your right, is a pair of stone pillars that mark the entrance to the Fitch Natural History Reservation. Turn in here, and follow the drive until you see a sign and parking area.

Fitch Nature Trail

Ask anyone who took basic biology classes during the past five decades at the University of Kansas about the Fitch Natural History Reservation, and you are likely to be regaled with stories about the first time he or she touched a snake or heard a red-tailed hawk scream or became aware of the different kinds of woods and grasslands. The former student will surely remember Dr. Henry S. Fitch, the scientist who introduced them to these natural wonders.

Since KU established this reserve in 1948, Doctor Fitch has lived and worked here, studying the area, writing about it, and

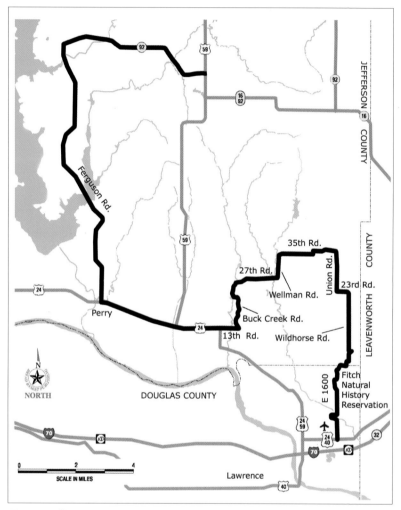

Tour 7: Jefferson County.

teaching many thousands of students to appreciate it. Now there's a marked trail that is open to the public, so that everyone can enjoy this favorite KU field trip.

Before you begin, it is helpful to brush up on the ecological concept called "succession," because that is one of the chief areas of study at the reserve. Basically, the succession theory holds that communities of plants change gradually over time in response to small changes in environmental conditions. Those changes allow new species to invade the site, and these changes continue to occur until finally the plants reach a "climax community" that is stable.

The plant communities of Jefferson County provide a vivid example of succession. Before white settlement, this land was mostly tallgrass prairie, with a few patches of oak-hickory forest on the uplands, and floodplain forest along the streams and rivers. Fires that regularly swept the prairie burned off woody shrubs and trees before they could get established, but the deep-rooted prairie grasses came back every year and thrived in the full-sun conditions they require.

When white settlers built towns and farms on the prairies, fires were no longer allowed to burn unchecked. Woody species such as honey locust and Osage orange got established, and they, in turn, created shade that hampered the growth of the grasses. As the trees got bigger, the ground got more shaded, which allowed the germination of still more species, until the grasses were gone and the biggest trees—the oaks and hickories—took over.

The beauty of the Henry S. Fitch Nature Trail is that you can see these different phases of succession up close. Imagine that these hills were nothing but grassland a hundred years ago. As you walk down the trail, you will come to an area in the early stage of succession, a scrubby woodland with Osage orange, cedars, and honey locusts. A bit farther along the trail, you will find some saplings of oak and hickory mixed in with the smaller trees. Farther still, you will find mature oaks and hickories shading out aging and spindly honey locusts and shrubs. Eventually, you will walk through a grove of tall black oaks with sparse undergrowth, an example of the oak-hickory climax forest that is found along the eastern edge of Kansas and eastward to the Atlantic coast.

Be sure to pick up a leaflet at the trailhead to take along on your hike. You can choose from two trails, the Biology Trail (where all those students hiked) at 0.8 miles, and the Upper Loop at 1.3 miles. Take the Upper Loop if you want to see the climax forest.

As you walk, you will see sheets of corrugated metal lying here and there on the ground. Doctor Fitch left these sheets to

Kaw Valley geology

The area's geologic history began a billion years ago, with metamorphic and igneous rocks that underlie the entire state but are not visible on the surface. On top of those rocks are layers of sediment put down by shallow seas that rose and fell over time.

About 300 million years ago, another oscillating sea covered the area, leaving behind layers of shale and limestone. Then, about a million years ago, glaciers moved down from the north, extending approximately to the Kansas River on the south and the Big Blue River on the west. As the glacier crept across northeast Kansas, it ground the earth into clay and silt, and carried big red quartzite boulders from Minnesota and South Dakota.

When the earth warmed and the glacier retreated, winds whipped up the deposited sediments and dropped them over the land. Since then, erosion caused by wind, rain, and rivers has cut into the surface of the land, creating hills and valleys.

If you were to fly over eastern Kansas looking for patterns, you would notice that this part of the state is a series of hills with a sharp faces, or escarpments, on the east, and gentle dipping slopes on the west. These hills are called the Osage cuestas, for the Spanish word for slope. Outcrops of erosion-resistant limestone cause the sharp slopes; the gentle slopes to the west are eroded layers of shale.

attract snakes and other reptiles. Don't pick them up unless you are prepared to meet a snake up close. When a class of students visits, Doctor Fitch can usually lift a sheet of metal and find some specimens to talk about. Seventeen species of snake are found here, but most are not venomous.

If you are mortally afraid of snakes, come in winter when they are hibernating in the limestone outcrops on the hillsides. At

Grazed Prairie

Grazing by cattle during the summer results in moderate to heavy brush and weed invasion.

Trees and brush encroach on grazed prairie, as shown at the Rockefeller tract.

other times of year, use snake smarts: wear long pants and leather boots, look before you step over logs or big rocks, and don't stick your hands under anything. Snakes are shy and will do all they can to get out of your way before you even see them. They are likely to bite only if you surprise them.

Prairie treatments

As you leave the Fitch Natural History Reservation, continue north on E. 1600 Road. After entering Jefferson County, the name of the road changes to Wild Horse Road. On your left, you will encounter the Rockefeller Experimental Tract, another of the Kansas Ecological Reserves.

This piece of land has been divided into four treatments that have been maintained since 1962 to determine the best way to maintain a prairie. The parcel that had nothing done to it is now a scrubby woodland. The parcel that was mowed is clear of trees, but the quality of the grass isn't high. Finally, you will come to a thriving, lush plot of tallgrass prairie. That plot has been burned periodically, proving that fire is good for the prairie. (For more

The Rockefeller Experimental Tract demonstrates that burned prairie stays healthy and vigorous, without incursions of woody plants.

information on prairie burns, see Chapter 10 on the Konza Prairie near Manhattan.)

Continue north on Wild Horse Road until it ends at a stop sign; straight ahead and to your right is a line of sycamore trees bordering Pony Creek. Farther up the creek on private property is a great blue heron rookery, big nests of sticks high up in the sycamores. Although you can't see the nests, you may see herons flying to and fro in spring as they bring food to their young.

Turn left on 23rd Street, then right on Union Road, going north, and follow it as it turns west and becomes 35th Street. On your left you will pass a gate entrance for the Circle S Ranch, where a country inn sits just beyond your view. This property and the adjoining S-Bar-S Ranch are the largest remaining pieces of prairie in the county.

Ranchers use these prairie lands for raising cattle and buffalo, which sometimes graze where you can see them from the road. When you imagine this area before white settlement, this is the

picture you should have in mind—rolling hills of grass with lines
of tall timber down in the creek valleys.

Buck Creek Scenic Road

When the road ends at Wellman Road, go left, then right
again on 27th Street, which will take you across Mud Creek and
into the beautiful Buck Creek Valley. For early settlers to Jefferson
County, this was the place to stake a claim if you wanted to farm.
Much of the bottomland along the creek is still used for raising
crops. The hilly landscape of Jefferson County, like the rest of the
Kaw Valley, reveals millions of years of geologic history.

Turn left on Buck Creek Road, which will wind along beside
Buck Creek. The road will fork where it ends at 13th Street. Take
the right fork, and follow 13th Street to its end on U.S. 24.

On your right, you will see a renovated one-room schoolhouse. Buck Creek School was built in 1878 of native limestone

The Buck Creek School has been renovated but is not open to the public.

and served this area for 74 years, until consolidation moved the students into a bigger regional school in 1952. Many one-room schoolhouses that dotted the landscape are rotting away, but the owners of this property have preserved the exterior of Buck Creek School. It is not currently used, however, and is not open to the public. Schoolhouses are an exceedingly common sight on the rural roads of Kansas. (For more information about their numbers and history, see Chapter 9, Skyline Drive.)

Perry Lake

Go west on U.S. 24 and north on Ferguson Road toward Perry Lake. This is another big U.S. Army Corps of Engineers reservoir, built between 1964 and 1969 on the Delaware River. It is

Grasshopper Falls

When this area was settled in the 1850s, the river was called Grasshopper River, and the town north of the lake, now called Valley Falls, was called Grasshopper Falls. No doubt the settlers were mildly amused by the number and size of grasshoppers found in the area. But after residents recognized grasshoppers as a serious threat to farms and gardens, they changed the town and river names.

Grasshopper plagues occurred during the severe drought of 1874 and 1875. Hordes of the insects would sweep into an area like a black cloud and eat virtually everything in sight before moving on. Grasshoppers reduced crops to stubble, laid gardens bare, stripped laundry from clotheslines, and devoured curtains. The grasshoppers were worse in western Kansas than here, and the settlers in western Kansas, being new to the area, were ill-prepared for any setbacks.

The Legislature convened a special session to pass legislation allowing counties to issue bonds to help people, and relief agencies were called to aid Kansas. People in other states sent money, food, and clothes to help the grasshopper-destroyed areas survive.

managed in conjunction with Milford, Tuttle Creek, and Clinton reservoirs to provide flood protection on the Kansas River. The dam is off to your left, but continue north and follow the signs to the Slough Creek area, where you will find several excellent hiking trails.

The first trailhead, on your left as you drive into the area, is called Thunder Ridge Nature Trail. It is 3 miles long and has 30 educational stations. Pick up the brochure at the trailhead that explains the features you will be viewing. The educational stations are geared to middle-school-aged children, but even adults will appreciate the gentle interpretation.

A bit farther down the road is a trailhead for the Perry Lake Trail, a 30-mile National Recreation Trail that winds up and down the hills and valleys on the east side of the lake. It traverses many kinds of landscapes, including prairies, farm fields, upland woodlands, intermittent streams, and riparian areas. A brochure at the trailhead will point out some of these features. If the trail is too muddy, you can hike along the sandy shore of the lake.

Oskaloosa

Take Kansas 92 east into the town of Oskaloosa. The county seat of Jefferson County, Oskaloosa lacks the ornate courthouse found in most other counties. The fancy Jefferson County Courthouse of 1867 was destroyed by a tornado in 1960. Oskaloosa was a progressive town in the 19th century; despite the fact that women could not vote in national or state elections, they could hold local office, and they did so here. The mayor and all five council members in 1888 were women.

If you are here on a weekend, be sure to visit Old Jefferson Town. It's a collection of historic buildings — not reproductions — that were moved from various places in Jefferson County. There is a schoolhouse, church, jail, and blacksmith shop. You can also visit the boyhood home of artist John Steuart Curry, which features a nice collection of reproductions of his famous paintings. Outside, there is a 4-acre reseeded prairie with a walking trail.

An old schoolhouse is among the historic buildings at Old Jefferson Town.

From here, go south on U.S. 59. When you reach the intersection with U.S. 24, you will be at the first white residence in Kansas, which was established in 1827 by Major Daniel Morgan Boone, son of the famous Kentucky pioneer Daniel Boone. The younger Boone was sent here to teach the Kansa Indians to farm. He took 100 acres on Schoolhouse Creek and raised his family here.

For more information

- Perry Lake U.S. Army Corps of Engineers office, 10419 Perry Park Drive, Perry, KS 66073; 785-597-5144.
- Perry State Park, 5441 West Lake Rd., Ozawkie, KS 66070; 785-246-3449.
- Jefferson County Economic Development Commission, P.O. Box 104, Oskaloosa, KS 66066; 785-863-3072.

Topeka to Tuttle Creek

This tour will focus on early white settlement and the Oregon Trail. You will travel some gravel roads and get out of your car often to hike and inspect several old grave sites, so wear appropriate clothing.

We will begin in the capital city, but we won't stay long. Most Kansans have seen the sights in Topeka, but, if you haven't, make plans to return and spend a day. The Capitol, with murals by John Steuart Curry and a renovated Senate chamber, should be your first stop. Gage Park, with a restored carousel, mini-train, and zoo, is a wonderful place for children, and flower lovers will enjoy the extensive rose garden. Historic Ward-Meade Park boasts a Victorian mansion, 2.5 acres of botanical gardens, a log cabin, and a

The Kansas Historical Society Museum is among sites of interest in Topeka.

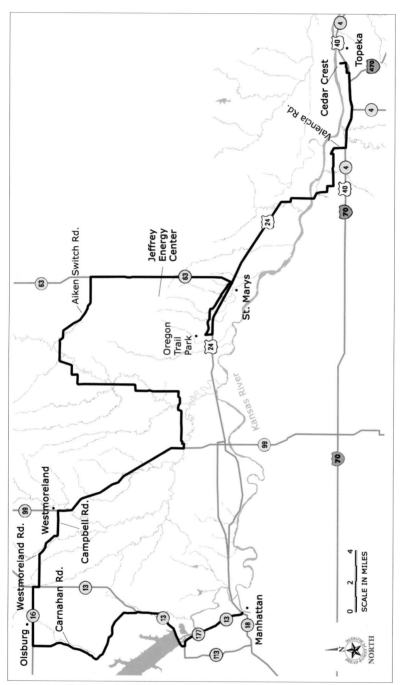

Tour 8: Topeka to Tuttle Creek.

replica of a prairie town. The Brown vs. Board of Education National Historic Site explains the city's role in school desegregation. And the Kansas History Museum is excellent; kids especially love it for such full-size artifacts as an 1880s train, a tipi and grass lodge, and a covered wagon. For a complete list of Topeka attractions, contact the Convention and Visitor's Bureau (details at end of this chapter).

Cedar Crest Wildlife Habitat and Jogging Trail

Begin at the governor's mansion, called Cedar Crest, where you will find a trail winding through 200 acres of wildlife habitat. Flat, paved parts of the trail run adjacent to Interstate 70 and are pretty noisy, but there is some lovely woodland walking where you can forget you are at the edge of the city.

Park on the west side of the governor's mansion to find the trailhead for the wooded area. The trail is interesting botanically because of its seamless transition from upland woodlands, with its complex of oaks and hickories, to the riparian area along the streams. See whether you can identify the trees in each area. (For more information on the two types of woodlands, see Chapter 3.)

The Oregon Trail

From here, the tour heads west from Topeka on Interstate 70. Get off at Exit 350, Valencia Road. Go north, and then turn left just before the railroad tracks. The road winds up a hill, and on your right near the top you will see an old stone octagonal building. This odd structure predates the Oregon Trail, and various reports indicate it was in use as a store and harness repair shop serving wagon trains heading west. It is on private property, however, so you can't go inspect it.

Devotees of Oregon Trail history have worked hard to find all the swales and ruts marking the trail's route and to preserve and erect signs on as much of it as possible. The Oregon-California Trails Association, founded in 1982, has more than 5,000 members devoted to the task, and the Kanza Chapter is one of the most active. You will see plenty of trail-related sites in this area, and you may even encounter some trail fans, books in hand, making the

Oregon Trail

After the Lewis and Clark expedition of 1806, Americans became aware of the fertile, free land in the place called Oregon. But the route taken by Lewis and Clark, up the Missouri River, seemed interminable, and only a few adventurers and traders made the trip. In 1819, Major Stephen H. Long made an expedition to the West and, upon his return, labeled the Great Plains "the great American desert," further discouraging travel.

Many people, disappointed in their fortunes in the United States and dreaming of something better in the West, nevertheless were waiting for news that the country could be traversed by wagon. Wagons were essential for migration, as they carried possessions, sheltered families during the trip, and provided housing at their destination until houses could be built.

In 1832, a caravan made it across the Great Plains and the mountains, to western Wyoming. In 1841, 60 men, women, and children in 13 wagons made it to Oregon. In 1842, John C. Fremont made the trip and provided maps of the route. The following year, 1,000 people emigrated to Oregon along the trail, and the "Great Migration" was on. By 1870, when the transcontinental railroad made the trail obsolete, as many as 200,000 people are estimated to have traveled the Oregon Trail to a new life in the West.

The trail started in Kansas City, Missouri, passed through Lawrence, and crossed the Kansas River in Topeka. The trail then went northwest to the Big Blue River in north-central Kansas and into Nebraska. The trail traversed Nebraska, Wyoming, Idaho, and Oregon before ending at the Willamette Valley south of what is now Portland, Oregon. The journey, which most settlers made on foot to spare their oxen, was 2,000 miles long and took five to six months.

full pilgrimage from Kansas City, Missouri, to the Columbia River near Portland, Oregon. To follow the trail closely takes three to four weeks of car travel, and many trail buffs do it.

Uniontown

Carry on down the hill, which generally follows the route of the Oregon Trail. On Gilkerson Street, you will see a sign for the Green Memorial Wildlife Area, where you can hike through the mosaic prairie and oak-hickory forest. Across the road is an old cemetery, all that remains of what was one of the largest settlements in Kansas in the 1850s. Called Uniontown, this was the official U.S. government trading post for the Pottawatomie Indian Reservation. The Pottawatomie were settled here in 1847 after they were forced off their lands in Indiana, Illinois, and Michigan. About 3,200 Pottawatomie Indians were living here by 1848.

At the same time, travel through here on the Oregon Trail was becoming heavy. A traveler in 1849 described Uniontown this way: "The trading post is a small hamlet composed of some half-dozen shops and a little straggling suburb of wigwams. The shops are kept by white men licensed to supply the Indians around with the flimsy, fantastic, and trumpery articles they require."

In 1849, a cholera epidemic struck Uniontown. Most of the white settlers fled, but among those who stayed were the doctor and his wife, and they both contracted it and died. The Pottawatomie were particularly hard hit, and at least 22 were found dead in the streets. The few whites who remained burned Uniontown to the ground.

The next year, Uniontown was reestablished with 50 new buildings, including 14 stores, which made it the biggest settlement for miles. In 1852, the paymaster was robbed of $20,000 in gold. U.S. Dragoons killed the robbers, but the gold was never recovered. After 1854, Uniontown's influence began to wane as Topeka grew. In 1859, it was abandoned and again burned to the ground.

In 1861, when Kansas became a state, the size of the Pottawatomie Reservation was drastically reduced to an 11-square-mile area carved from the corner of the original reservation, about

Cholera

Cholera was a terrible reality for travelers in 1849. It struck and took its victims quickly; many people experienced a stomach ache in the morning and death by evening. During the Gold Rush, many travelers were young men going alone. If cholera struck one of these men, the party would leave him and his mule by the side of the road. If he recovered, he might catch up; if not, he would die where he lay.

Families would carry their dead along with them until the end of the day. Then, a shallow grave would be dug at the head of the trail, so that the entire caravan would roll over it the next morning, erasing any trace that might attract wild animals to dig up the body.

12 miles north of what was Uniontown. The reservation remains there today.

River crossing

Leaving the cemetery, you will travel into the town of Willard and cross the Kansas River. The Kaw was one of the first dangers travelers faced on the Oregon Trail. Most left Independence, Missouri, on the five-month journey in spring so they could get to the other side of the mountains before winter. But in spring, the Kaw was treacherous; in those days before dams upstream controlled the flow, the Kaw could become a roiling, angry river.

Several entrepreneurs made a good livelihood helping the travelers across. Most crossed at Pappan's Ferry in what is now downtown Topeka. The Pappan brothers' ferry boat in 1843 consisted of three dugout canoes supporting a single deck, and they charged $1 per wagon to cross. By 1849, the brothers had two boats in operation, each able to carry two wagons. They lowered the wagons to the river with ropes and had a team of oxen on the other side to pull them out. For the extra service, they raised their price to $4 a wagon.

In 1849, a Missouri newspaper reported that when the Kansas River was high, travelers would find an excellent ford at Uniontown. Thousands of emigrants bypassed Pappan's Ferry at Topeka and headed 15 miles west for this location, which became known as the Upper Kansas Crossing.

The Kansas river crossing, eight days out of Independence, became the traditional place where wagon trains reorganized, tightened discipline, and elected leaders. At a given signal, men who wanted to lead the journey would march across the prairie, and the travelers would run behind the candidate of their choice. The man with the longest tail of people following him was thus elected.

At least two ferries began operating near the current bridge over the Kaw at Uniontown, and each was said to carry 65 to 70 wagons per day. At $1 per wagon, the ferry operators made a handsome wage for the time.

St. Mary's

After you've crossed the river into Rossville, turn west on U.S. 24. As you arrive in the town of St. Mary's, the town's most obvious landmark—the impressive hillside buildings of St. Mary's College and Academy—will be on your right. You are welcome to walk around the campus, but the buildings are not open to the public.

St. Mary's is a Catholic school, both day school and boarding school for children, and it has a small liberal-arts college. But it is unlike any other Catholic college in the United States. Its uniqueness lies in the fact that it belongs to the Society of St. Pius X, an offshoot of the Catholic Church that rejected modern reforms undertaken during the past three decades. In this traditionalist community, the Mass is said in Latin, boys and girls are separated for their schooling, nuns wear full habits, and college students must adhere to strict dress codes—jacket and tie for men, skirts two inches below the knee for women.

Few of the students here are natives of this area, but many traditionalist Catholics from across the country have moved here so that their children may attend. The Society of St. Pius X pur-

The Boys Dormitory remains in use at St. Mary's College and Academy.

chased the property in 1978, after it had stood empty for more than a decade. In the fall of that year, the beautiful Immaculata Chapel, built in 1909, burned. Members of the church are slowly restoring the chapel, sorting and numbering rocks to reassemble the walls.

Before its present use, St. Mary's was a Jesuit seminary for 36 years, and before that, a Catholic college. Its history, however, goes back to the very beginnings of white settlement in Kansas. In 1848, a Catholic mission to the Pottawatomie was established here. Father Gailland, one of the founders, described their beginnings:

"Primitive conditions faced the new arrivals. About a hundred yards apart from each other stood two log buildings nearly identical in form. No doors were hung, no windows in place. The chinks between the logs were not caulked. There were no articles of furniture or other accommodations, excepting those which they had brought with them. The food supply consisted of a sack of cornmeal. At this point, the pioneer group of St. Mary's was left alone to face the grim winter. It will suffice to say that for 80 days teams and wagons could cross the river on the ice."

Indians came to the mission, willing to enroll their children in the school, but in 1849, cholera arrived here, too. The Indians, who already knew the deadly effects of the disease, fled the mission, and the priests spent their time attending to the sick and dying. In the spring of that year, gold-seeking forty-niners passed through here in droves on their way to California.

In the next decade, St. Mary's became famous among the emigrants on the Oregon trail as the last bastion of civilization before the wilderness. One traveler in 1850 described it this way: "It is a neat looking place, consisting of three or four two-story log houses belonging to the church and about 20 small log huts. The Indians here have large farms and seem to be very industrious."

In 1850, the Vatican appointed Bishop John Miege as Vicar of the Indian Territory. In 1852, he wrote that there were 3,500 Pottawatomie living in small villages over 30 square miles, and he considered 1,500 of them to be converted to Catholicism. But the Indians were dispersed when the reservation was broken up in 1861, some moving to the smaller reservation to the northeast, and some moving to Oklahoma. St. Mary's then began its life as a college.

Oregon Trail Park

Go five miles west of St. Mary's on U.S. 24, and turn right on Oregon Trail Road, following the signs for Oregon Trail Park. You will know you are there when you see a silo painted with scenes from the Oregon Trail. This is a great place to have a picnic and let the kids run. There are restrooms and a picnic shelter, two short trails, and a third trail that is almost a mile long.

The long trail, called the Sea of Grass Trail, takes you to the top of a hill that overlooks the Jeffrey Energy Center, a big coal-burning power plant. Western Resources, the company that owns the power plant, also owns this park. The view of the river valley to the south is more serene.

Wind power

Go back to St. Mary's, and take U.S. 63 north. We are going

Scenes from the Oregon Trail cover a silo in Oregon Trail Park.

to be making a big loop, some of it on gravel roads, around the Jeffrey Energy Center and into ranching country. The power plant, operating since 1978, has three coal-burning generating units.

You will notice two wind turbines on the hilltop; they are part of a pilot project to test the feasibility of using wind power to generate electricity. Kansas is ranked as the state with the third best wind-power potential, after North Dakota and Texas. The turbines are mounted on 170-foot towers and each rotor blade is 75 feet long. The turbines have automatic sensors that detect wind direction and speed so that they can face into the wind and vary blade pitch based on wind speed. The turbines start producing electricity when the wind speed is 9 mph and stop when it exceeds 65 mph. The turbines generate 3.6 million kilowatts a year, enough to power about 400 households. Western Resources is building an information kiosk north of the plant, so watch for signs if you want to learn more about the wind project.

Jeffrey Energy Center is open to the public for wildlife viewing on its three lakes and three wildlife management areas. During the spring and fall migrations, you might see geese, ducks, common mergansers, and double-crested cormorants. Osprey and bald eagles are occasionally sighted fishing in the lakes, and large numbers of snow geese winter here.

Cattle ranching

About four miles north of the power plant, turn left on Aiken Switch Road. This is a gravel road that runs beside the railroad tracks for a few miles. You will quickly realize that these tracks are well-used; this is the Union Pacific Railroad line from Wyoming. More than 50 trains come through here every day, most of them 150-car coal trains. One or two go to the Jeffrey Energy Center, and most continue on to other power plants.

Coal is the main business for the railroad now, but years ago, cattle were more important. Unlike the Kansas River bottomlands just 12 miles south, this land is not suitable for crops. The hills are too steep, and the soil is too thin and rocky. This ground grows great grass, though, and that means a rancher could make a good livelihood in these hills, given enough acreage. Most of the land you will be crossing belongs to just a few ranchers—a 10,000-acre ranch here is not uncommon.

As the road parallels the rail line, watch for an old railroad corral on your left, a wooden system of chutes and pens where cattle were moved on and off trains in the heyday of the range-fed cattle business. Most of the old railroad corrals are long gone, burned up in the grass fires sparked by passing trains. This one, so far, has remained intact.

Today, trucks bring cattle to these hills. Just-weaned calves are fed grain for about four months through the winter, then put out on grass in April or May, where they graze for three months. Then for about 100 days the cattle go off to a feedlot, where they gain three pounds a day before slaughter.

Cattle ranchingtakes advantage of prairie grasses, one of few "crops" suitable for the thin rocky soil in Kansas hills.

Railroads

Railroads played an important role in the settlement of Kansas. The Pacific Railway Act of 1862 gave almost 4 million acres of land to the Kansas Pacific Railroad, which built its main line from Kansas City, Missouri, to Denver, much of it right beside the Kansas River. Because most land in the eastern half of the state was already claimed by then, most of the railroad grants were in western Kansas.

The Kansas Pacific, which later merged with the Union Pacific, aggressively promoted the sale and settlement of those lands so that the railroad would have a population to serve. The KP published a quarterly newsletter that circulated to 80,000 people touting the beauty and bounty of western Kansas. "Good soil for wheat, corn and fruit," trumpeted an early ad for settlers to southwest Kansas.

At the time, a quasi-scientific theory held that "rain follows the plow." People observed that here in eastern Kansas, early settlers had quickly changed the empty prairie into verdant farmland.

The theory was that when the prairie sod was plowed, the exposed soil could absorb more water, which would in turn foster evaporation and the formation of clouds, producing more rain and a more hospitable climate. The idea attracted many supporters, including Ferdinand V. Hayden, director of the U.S. Geological and Geophysical Survey in the Territories.

The railroads seized on the idea and promoted it throughout the East and in Europe. They offered free or reduced train fare to those who would settle in the West. Thousands did but, of course, the theory was nonsense, and when drought returned to the Plains in the 1870s, many settlers in both western and eastern Kansas gave up and moved back East.

More Oregon Trail

Follow Onaga Road south, and turn right on Oregon Trail Road. Stop at the historical marker, and visit the cemetery. The tall gravestone is that of Louis Vieux, a Pottawatomie chief who was given an allotment of land on Red Vermillion Creek in 1857. He bought the bridge over the creek and charged Oregon Trail travelers a $1 toll to cross. On the road, just before you reach the bridge, you will see a white gate with a faded sign. Walk down the path to the Red Vermillion crossing, the steep banks of which made this a particularly difficult crossing for immigrants who came through before Louis Vieux's bridge was built.

Here is the site of one of the great tragedies of the Oregon Trail. Late in May 1849, a large party of immigrants was camped here when cholera struck. About 50 people were believed to have died here; only two graves have been located and marked.

Across the bridge is the remains of the Louis Vieux Elm, once the largest elm tree in the United States. Lightning and winds demolished it in the 1980s.

When Oregon Trail Road ends, go north on Kansas 99. Just before you reach Westmoreland, you will see the Scott Springs Oregon Trail Park with the covered wagon sculpture by local artist Ernest White. Trail ruts and a path lead down to the creek, where more graves have been located and marked.

In Westmoreland, you can see a deep hand-dug well, or visit the community museum. When you are ready to leave town, turn west on Campbell, which will take you past the Westmoreland Cemetery, which has one flagpole for every veteran who is buried there. The road becomes Westmoreland Road. Take it to Kansas 13 and go north briefly, then turn west on Kansas 16.

Flint Hills

Just east of Olsburg, go south on Carnahan Road, which traverses some superb tallgrass prairie. This is the northern edge of the Flint Hills, a 60-mile-wide band of hilly tallgrass prairie that runs south into Oklahoma.

Much of this land is maintained in tallgrass prairie by fires set every year or two to kill invading woody species. A Flint Hills fire is an awe-inspiring sight even today, when you know that the fires are being managed and that roads will let you quickly escape them. Imagine how the Oregon Trail travelers and early settlers felt when a natural fire spread across the prairie.

The land on the east side of the road is privately owned, but there is some public access on the west where you can wander down into the valley of what used to be the Big Blue River. Today, the river is impounded to form Tuttle Creek Lake.

Tuttle Creek

Carnahan Road will end at Kansas 13; continue south but do not cross the dam. Follow the signs to Rocky Ford, where you are likely to find dozens of people fishing if the weather is nice. Rocky Ford was the site of a grist mill and later a hydroelectric plant on the Big Blue River as early as the 1870s. It has long been considered one of the best places in the area to catch catfish. Newspaper accounts from 1870 report on people who caught up to 400 pounds of fish in one trip.

Rocky Ford now is just below the Tuttle Creek dam, so the water level can rise suddenly when water is released upstream. A siren is supposed to sound before that happens, but be aware that any sudden increase in water level means you should head back to higher ground.

Next stop is Tuttle Creek State Park—River Pond Area. The dam was built in 1962 to control flooding on the Big Blue and Kansas rivers. During wet periods, the reservoir can more than quadruple in size to alleviate flooding downstream, and during dry periods, it can be managed to improve water quality in the Kansas River and aid navigation in the Missouri River.

Tuttle Creek got its first serious test in 1993, when heavy spring rainfall caused flooding throughout the Midwest. Tuttle Creek held back as much water as it could hold—61 feet above its normal pool—and then the spillway gates had to be opened to release some water. The 18 gates were raised, and the torrent that roared through the spillway scoured a canyon that unearthed all kinds of fossils and interesting geological formations. The Corps of Engineers has since filled in that canyon.

From here, you can cross the dam and go south on Kansas 177 to Manhattan and Interstate 70.

For more information

- Topeka Convention and Visitors Bureau, 800-235-1030; www.topekacvb.org.
- Western Resources' Jeffrey Energy Center Wind project: http://www.wstnres.com/wind_generation.html.
- Tuttle Creek U.S. Army Corps of Engineers, 785-539-8511.
- Tuttle Creek State Park, 785-539-7941.

Skyline Drive to Alma and Wamego

This tour focuses on Flint Hills ranching and small-town life. Although the Flint Hills are far above the Kansas River, they are part of the Kaw watershed. And though the landscape on this trip feels much different from that in previous tours, you will never be more than 15 miles from the river. This trip involves a lot of driving, much of it on gravel roads, and some walking in towns. It's not strenuous, and no special clothes or equipment are needed. You may want to take a camera, though, for the splendid vistas and wildflowers you will encounter on this route.

Skyline-Mill Creek Drive

The state has identified this drive from Interstate 70 to Alta Vista as a scenic road. The first half features a stretch of ridge top through tallgrass prairie, and the second half follows the Mill Creek valley. On this tour, we are going to do only the first part, the Skyline portion, but if you want to spend a full day, you can wander down the second half of the road and then take major highways to pick up the rest of this tour.

Leave I-70 at Exit 335, Snokomo Road, and head south. For the first few miles the road winds through the Snokomo Creek valley, its meanders marked by thin borders of trees and surrounded by flat crop land. Gradually, the road turns east and then south again, rising higher into the hills.

The first landmark you will come to is the Snokomo School House, which has a state historic plaque beside it. The well pump in front works, and local residents and sightseers often use it. You are welcome to walk around and look in the windows. This school lasted until 1941, when its students were transferred to a new consolidated district in Alma.

One-room schoolhouses were common throughout the rural landscape until just a few decades ago. At the turn of the twentieth century, Kansas had 9,284 school districts, each with its own schoolhouse; Wabaunsee County alone had 88 schoolhouses. School districts were consolidated in the 1960s, bringing the number of districts in the state down to 311 by 1969.

Most one-room schoolhouses fell into disrepair or were torn down. The Snokomo School House was lucky; a local civic group, "The Silent Workers," decided to restore it in 1972. As it turned

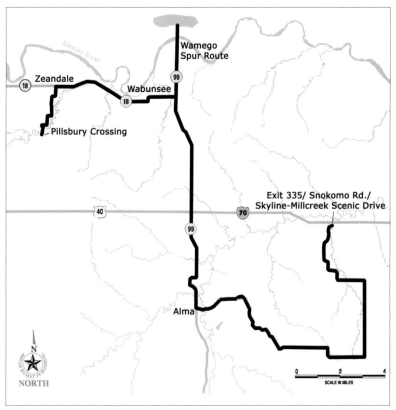

Tour 9: Skyline Drive to Alma and Wamego.

out, the building had to be restored a second time, after a tornado took off the roof, bell tower, chimney, window panes, and part of the back wall in April 1991. In 1995, the schoolhouse was placed on the National Register of Historic Places.

Minutes from meetings of the Snokomo School Board exist back to the 1860s, and they provide a pretty good picture of education in those days. Each school district was governed by a three-member school board, whose primary job was to hire the teacher. Rural school boards preferred to hire men, at least for the winter term. They thought male teachers would be more able to control the older farm boys, who attended school in winter when they had less farm work to do at home. Male teachers were routinely paid more than women. In 1877, A.F. Wade, a man, got $33 a month to teach the winter semester here, and Katie Cotton got $25 a month for the summer semester.

The length of the school year depended on how much money the school district had to pay the teacher. District records show

One-room schoolhouses, such as this one at Snokomo, are common across the Kaw Valley countryside.

that the school board scheduled six months of school in 1893, but noted that the school year would run longer if more money could be found. In general, schools operated seven months a year.

There were no compulsory education laws until the early 1900s, so local districts were on their own in deciding educational policies. This school enrolled people over 21 years old until 1890, when the board decided to limit attendance to children. Epidemics and bad weather cut into the school year frequently, and many children attended sporadically because they were needed at home.

Even so, the illiteracy rate in Kansas between 1870 and 1900 was less than 3 percent. Clearly, learning occurred when students were in school. The curriculum in 1890 was reading, grammar, arithmetic, geography, history, and physiology.

West along the ridge

When you reach the four-way stop sign (the FMV Ranch is straight ahead of you), turn right. The road leads west and ascends a ridge where you will be surrounded by tallgrass prairie. Imagine yourself as an 1850s settler, bouncing up this hill with your children and all your earthly goods in the wagon behind you. Imagine cutting through grass that in wet years could be 10 feet tall. You probably would be arriving in spring, when the grass was a tangle of brilliant green, splashed with the colors of wildflowers.

When you get to the top of the ridge and get your first vista of the Flint Hills stretching away to the west, imagine what this view must have meant to the early settlers. Surely they saw opportunity as they looked off into the distance, into the empty hills, cut by streams and bordered by ribbons of flat, fertile bottom ground. They had left behind the civilized east, where it was increasingly difficult to buy land and make a livelihood, and set off with dreams of building prosperous farms for themselves.

As you drive along this road, you will notice loading pens at nearly every driveway, a sure sign that most people who live here today are raising cattle. But cattle ranching was something of an afterthought for early settlers. Most who came here from the East or from Europe expected to be farmers as they had been previ-

Cattle pens near driveways indicate that ranching is an economic mainstay.

ously, and they staked their claims along the streams. They grew grains and vegetables, established orchards and vineyards, raised sheep and milk cows and poultry.

But as you can see at a glance, the bottomland where diversified farming was possible is just a tiny portion of the landscape here. By 1907, more and more farmers were renting out their upper pastures to graze cattle brought from Texas. At first, cattle provided a small supplemental income, but over time they became an ever greater portion of a farmer's livelihood.

A few miles farther along, you will come to what looks like a big white soccer ball on a metal tower. That's a "radome," or Doppler radar tower, used to detect radial motion of the airflow within a storm, which gives weather experts a better chance of predicting tornadoes. These are popping up increasingly in rural areas, as television stations erect their own towers so they can do their own forecasting, part of the competitive TV news business.

As you begin to descend from the ridge, you will notice the road is paved for a short distance. Look at the land beside the road, and you will understand why. This is a ridge of crumbling rocks that would be difficult to get across if it weren't paved. Those crumbling rocks also explain why the Flint Hills retain the largest remaining areas of tallgrass prairie in the United States: The terrain is no good for farming. Elsewhere, prairie was plowed for crop land and paved over for cities, but in these rocky hills, neither was possible.

On your right as you come down the hill is a pipe spouting water into a trough; it's one of the many springs found in the Flint Hills. Underground streams erupt from hillsides in many locations, providing cool, clean water for cattle and cattle hands. Groundwater also seeps out of rocks below escarpments in some places, providing enough water to support shrubs and small trees. That is why you often see a horizontal line of shrubs just below the top of a hill that is otherwise covered with grass.

At the bottom of the hill, you will cross Mill Creek. Where the road ends, turn right, and go into Alma.

Alma

Pull into a parking spot on the main street, and take a stroll through the business district, where you will see many superb examples of the stonecutter's art. Browse the Wabaunsee County Historical Museum, where you may find a quilting bee in progress. One block west is the Wabaunsee County Courthouse (ironically, built of Indiana limestone rather than the beautiful golden local stone), two nineteen-century stone churches, and many beautiful old homes.

With a current population of 900, Alma has held its own for more than a century, surviving several economic boom-and-bust cycles. It is close enough to Topeka and Manhattan that many residents commute to jobs there. But it is far enough away that it has avoided the bland suburbanization that afflicts so many towns nearer to cities. With its wide, clean streets and warm limestone buildings, Alma has preserved its charm and its heritage.

Alma was incorporated in 1868 by its 13 inhabitants, and its population grew quickly. The town had several forays into industry that residents at the time hoped would turn their farm-focused village into a city. In 1874, oil was found in a newly dug well—

The pipe carries spring water to a cattle tank.

many later believed oil had been poured in as a practical joke—
and townspeople quickly formed a company and put a drilling rig
into action.

They never found oil, but they did find salt water, so they
constructed a salt works, with 25 big kettles to boil the brine. In
1877, the Alma Salt Works produced 30 to 50 barrels of pure white
salt per day. Within five years, though, it shut down because the
price of fuel to boil the water was too high.

In June 1880, the Manhattan, Alma, and Burlingame Railroad reached Alma, and residents expected their town to boom.
Their mayor formed a company to explore for coal, and stone quar-
rying thrived. But the town got too optimistic and invested too
much in the coal mines, which never produced much. The bank
failed, bonds were called, and taxes had to be raised to pay off the
debt. Throughout it all, though, Alma retained a sense of community pride that remains obvious today.

Still, it struggles with the two forces that empty small towns
throughout rural Kansas: an aging population and a lack of economic opportunity for young people. Ranching, fortunately, is
somewhat profitable at the moment, buying more time for the

German settlers

When the Kansas-Nebraska Act opened the Kansas Territory to land claims in 1854, eastern Kansas was snapped up by people on both sides of the slavery issue. (See Chapter 5 for more information about the slavery issue.) Meanwhile, many Germans were heading for the United States to escape the political and military oppression of Chancellor Otto von Bismarck. Between 1830 and 1870, at least 2 million Germans emigrated to the States, and some came to Kansas.

Typical of them was Frederick Palenske, who in the spring of 1854 left Bremen, Germany, with his wife and baby and sailed for New Orleans. They took a steamship up the Mississippi and Missouri rivers, then disembarked at Westport in what is now Kansas City, Missouri. They bought a wagon and provisions and set out in search of newly available land in Kansas Territory. In May 1855, they came through these hills and met a discouraged bachelor who had staked a claim and was living in a tent. He sold them his claim, tent and all, for $20. The Palenskes built a house, started a farm, and prospered. They lived on that land the rest of their lives, becoming some of the most prominent members of the community, and their descendants are still here.

Two German brothers, John and Peter Thoes, made their way to this area in the fall of 1854 and staked claims on the south branch of Mill Creek before heading to Kansas City for the winter. In the spring of 1855, they returned, bringing a brother-in-law with them, and built three log cabins on their claims. In April, John set off alone on the weeklong trip to Kansas City to get provisions. He found the town frenetic with activity. Immigrants on the Oregon Trail were gathering at Westport Landing, and settlers to Kansas and Nebraska territories were preparing for their trips into the wilderness.

Everywhere, people talked about settling, and the big question was, "Where can we find fertile land that hasn't been claimed yet?" As he waited in line for his provisions, he noticed a group of young men speaking his native tongue, so he approached them, and they asked the same question. He told them about Mill Creek, 120 miles west. The men, 30 in all, were scouting for land for the Cincinnati Colony, an Ohio group of Germans who hoped to move west and found a new town. The men held a quick conference and unanimously voted to go with Thoes to Mill Creek.

When they arrived, they selected a site just south of present Alma and laid out lots for a prospective town called Humboldt City. Each member of the party took several lots as his share of the venture, hoping to sell them to other members of the colony who would come later. As it turned out, no one was willing to pay the inflated prices for the town lots, and new arrivals staked their own claims farther west. The winter of 1856 was particularly cold and snowy in Kansas, and many of the Cincinnati Colony gave up and returned to Ohio.

Other German settlers, many fresh from Germany, had drifted into the area for a few years. They had to stay; home was 5,000 miles away, and they had no money to move back. In 1859 and 1860, nature again turned harsh, this time with drought, and the settlers suffered terribly. Churches and social agencies east of the Mississippi River called for donations for "Starving Kansas," and 8 million pounds of provisions and clothing, $85,000, and 2,500 bushels of seed wheat poured into the territory. In 1861, the year Kansas gained statehood, the weather turned around, and the harvest was bountiful.

In 1867, the federal government abolished the open range and offered farmers 40 cents a rod to build stone fences 4.5 feet tall. Two years later, a huge prairie fire 60 miles wide roared through this area from the Southwest, burning up many homes and barns but leaving the stone fences intact. From then on, settlers started using stone for all their building projects, and you still see many stone farmhouses and barns in this area.

many small towns in the Flint Hills that depend on the cattle economy for survival. Government business is another factor that keeps most county seats like Alma thriving.

Beecher Bible Church

Go north on Kansas 99; five miles past I-70, look on your right for a field of boulders called a *felsenmeer*, the German for "sea of rocks." Geologists believe the edge of the last glacier that covered northeast Kansas a million years ago left these rocks here. The glacier dragged boulders from the north, and when it began to melt, dropped them in this field. There are some boulders of red quartzite, now mostly covered with lichen, from South Dakota or Minnesota.

Go west on Kansas 18 to Wabaunsee, one of the most illustrious ghost towns in the state. In 1856, Charles Lines of New Haven, Connecticut, formed a colony to emigrate to Kansas Territory to fight for Kansas' admission to the nation as a free state. Nearly 100 people joined Lines, including a clergyman, physician, two former members of the Legislature, two theology students, and

The Beecher Bible and Rifle Church is named for the gift that Henry Ward Beecher made to the congregation.

many who had graduated from Yale.

Before their departure, the abolitionist preacher Henry Ward Beecher raised money to purchase 50 Sharps rifles. "Let these arms hang above your doors as the old Revolutionary muskets do in many New England dwellings," Beecher wrote. "May your children in another generation look upon them and say, 'Our father's courage saved this fair land from blood and slavery.'" The rifles were packed, along with bibles and hymnals, in boxes labeled "Beecher's Bibles."

When the settlers arrived here at Antelope Creek, they laid out a town site that included parks, land for a university, and space for the state capitol. They were convinced that Wabaunsee would become the New Haven of the West. Several times in 1856, the men at Wabaunsee came to the aid of abolitionists at Lawrence. And at the end of that year, Wabaunsee became a stop on the Underground Railroad, where slaves found refuge on their way to freedom in the north.

In 1862, the stone church that still stands was completed and named the Beecher Bible and Rifle Church. More settlers arrived, and the town prospered. But after the turn of the twentieth century, people began to leave Wabaunsee for the larger towns nearby, and Wabaunsee went into decline. In the 1920s, the church closed, but eventually was restored and reopened. Services are still held there every Sunday.

Pillsbury Crossing

Return to Kansas 18, and go west to Zeandale. Follow the signs down the gravel road to Pillsbury Crossing Wildlife Area. Here, Deep Creek cascades over a ledge of limestone about 40 feet wide. It is only a 5-foot drop, but that's about as big as the waterfalls get in this part of the state.

The creek's smooth rock bottom makes this a good place to wade when the water is low. Make sure you can see the rock clearly before letting children in, because high water can make this stream impassable. Also, be aware that the road crosses through the stream here, and some local people might drive

Pillsbury Crossing provides a rare Kansas waterfall for visitors' enjoyment.

through it. You may spot beaver activity in the creek or on the banks.

Least terns

Return to Kansas 99, and go north toward Wamego. When the land flattens and you see crop land, you will know you're again near the Kansas River. You will notice that the river bank appears pretty steep, and people have built houses right up to the river without benefit of a levy. In 1993, the most recent flood year, Wamego and other towns on the Kaw had to sandbag as the river rose but, fortunately, they did not get flooded.

One unexpected effect of the 1993 flood was the arrival of an endangered species, the least tern. This small, gull-like bird had suffered severe declines in numbers primarily because of habitat loss. The least tern needs sand islands and isolation from predators to nest. But for the past 50 years, America's streams and rivers have been increasingly controlled by dams and reservoirs, which prevent the natural cycle that creates sandbars and islands in low water and that scours them clear of vegetation in floods.

The floods of 1993 and 1995, however, were so powerful that they duplicated that natural cycle, leaving behind wide, sandy islands in the river. These sandbars were the perfect place for a tern to scratch out a hole and lay eggs, and for the next five years, 25 to 30 nesting pairs in four colonies were spotted on the Kaw between Manhattan and Topeka. Several of those colonies, particularly in the Wamego area, have produced young.

Sharing the sandbars are piping plovers, a threatened species that has the same nesting habits as the least tern. Having an endangered species never before known to nest on the Kaw was cause for celebration by naturalists. Anytime your state can give a boost to an endangered species, it is an honor.

Not everyone celebrated, though. Federal law says federal agencies must do all they can to help an endangered or threatened species, and in this case the federal agency most affected was the U.S. Army Corps of Engineers. The Corps operates Tuttle Creek Reservoir, which controls how much water flows through the Kaw here. To keep the terns' nests from being flooded, the Corps had to hold back more water in spring than it normally would, which meant the Tuttle Creek lake levels rose, which meant that boat docks were underwater.

Still, for the past several years, the Corps has controlled the flow from Tuttle Creek to accommodate the least tern. Whether that practice will continue is a subject of much discussion. The Corps has management plans for each of its reservoirs that try to satisfy competing interests relating to water flow, and the least tern may become a part of those management plans if it appears the species is here to stay.

Part of the decision hinges on whether studies show that it is safe for the terns to nest here. Much of the Kaw is restricted for fishing because the pesticide chlordane, a neurological poison and carcinogen, has been found in fish. Biologists hope to determine whether the least terns are ingesting chlordane when they fish these waters; if they are, the species is probably better off not living in the Kaw, and the river will not be managed to encourage them.

If you come to Wamego between April and early August, look out over the river. If you're lucky, you may be able to spot a snowy white bird with a black cap, soaring over the water on its way back from near-extinction.

Wamego

Continue north until you reach Wamego, a thriving town of 4,000 people. It was settled in 1866 by a group of seven men who set out from Topeka with the intention of starting a new town. Only one of the seven remained a permanent member, but other people were soon attracted to the lush bottomlands and orderly community.

John B. Schonhoff, an immigrant from Holland, bought a farm 12 miles north of the town and erected a windmill like the ones he knew back home. A pair of English stonemasons built the tower for the windmill from local yellow limestone, with a harder white limestone trim. For a few years, the Schonhoff family did custom grinding of feed and flour, but cattle, not grains, became the focus of the agricultural economy in this area. The mill was not a commercial success, and, by the late 1880s, the family had stopped operating it. It stood on their farm until 1924, when the second owner agreed to donate it to Wamego for use in its city park.

The windmill was disassembled, moved to town, and reassembled. It has been maintained by the city ever since, and provides a great backdrop for the city's Tulip Festival the third weekend of April. The mill is fully operational, and you can find flour ground there at local stores. The 12-acre park is a great place for children, and next door is a historical complex including a museum, one-room schoolhouse, jail, and log cabin. Bring a picnic!

On the main street in town is the Columbian Theatre, an amazing place for such a small community. But then, the man who brought it to Wamego was an amazing personality. J.C. Rogers, born in 1847, moved to Wamego in 1875 and opened a bank. Before long, he owned all the buildings on the west side of Lincoln Avenue between Fifth and Sixth streets. He was a quiet and frugal man, but a hard-headed one. At one point he became so angry at the Union Pacific Railroad for overcharging him $14 that he built his own line from Wamego to Wabaunsee to avoid giving the UP his business. He ran the freight line for three years until the railroad gave him back his $14. That same day, he shut down his line.

In 1893, Rogers and his wife, Mary Ann, were among a group of 1,500 people from this area who took the train to Chicago to see the Columbian Exposition and World's Fair. The fair celebrated the 400th anniversary of Columbus' discovery of America and attracted more than 27 million visitors—nearly half of the U.S. population—in the six months it was open. The "White City," as the fairgrounds were known, featured 200 buildings and pavilions on 633 acres in Chicago's Jackson Park. The spectacular architecture was reportedly the inspiration for the Emerald City in L. Frank Baum's Oz books.

Rogers was so taken with the fair that he returned to Chicago when the fair closed and purchased two complete buildings from the fair, plus many statues, paintings, and decorative pieces from other buildings. He reconstructed one building in Kansas City, Missouri, as a men's club (it was torn down in 1960 to make way for Interstate 35), another he sold to a friend, and he put many of the art pieces in storage.

Rogers had started construction of a new building on Lincoln Street in Wamego the previous year, and many of his art treasures were incorporated into its construction. The second-story windows were from the Brazil Pavilion at the exposition (designed by a team of architects that included the young Frank Lloyd Wright), and the tin eagle on the roof today came from the Government Building.

Four magnificent oil paintings by the German artist Earnest Theodor Behr were installed on the second floor. The paintings are similar to other allegorical art favored in Europe at that time, in which a woman was painted to represent an ideal such as liberty or justice. The women in these paintings celebrate material prosperity in America and represent the four regions of the country:

The Columbian Theater houses magnificent nineteenth-century paintings.

the shipping trade in the North, agriculture in the South and West, and arts and sciences in the East. The children in the paintings are similar to cherubs in Renaissance art, but they're hard at work. The diversity of the country is also noted, with figures of an African-American and Native Americans included.

As splendid as the theater was during Rogers' day, the true value of his acquisitions wasn't known until 1990, when Wamego residents decided to restore the theater. Beneath the stage they found a crate with 14 additional paintings from the exposition, including six with scenes of America: Washington, D.C., San Francisco, Niagara Falls, Yellowstone, Yosemite Valley, and Florida. These hung above the allegorical paintings in the Government Building at the exposition, and there had been eight such American scenes. It appears Rogers bought them all, but painted one silver to use as a silent movie screen; it appears to be a cityscape of Chicago but is not restorable. The restorers also found the top 8 inches of the final painting, fastened to a board; the canvas was no doubt sent to the dump long ago. The four paintings hanging in the Columbian today have been restored. The restoration of the others is planned for some time in the future.

The art works that Rogers took from the Columbian Exposition are the only known decorative art thought to have survived intact to this day. All the other pieces that were known to have been saved were stored in a building that fair sponsors planned to turn into a museum, but the building and its contents were destroyed by fire before that happened.

The Columbian Theatre is open for tours; you can also visit an art gallery and gift shop on the first floor. The theater is still used for theatrical and musical performances, so pick up a schedule. You may find yourself making plans to return to Wamego soon.

For more information:

✓ The Columbian Theatre, Museum, and Art Center, 521 Lincoln Ave, Wamego, KS 66547; 785-456-2029.

✓ Wamego Convention and Visitors Bureau, P.O. Box 34, Wamego, KS 66547; 785-456-7849; www.wamego.org.

Konza Prairie to Junction City

This tour involves quite a bit of hiking, so wear long pants and sturdy shoes, and bring your binoculars. It will focus on the natural history of the Flint Hills, with some white settlement history as a bonus.

Konza Prairie

From Interstate 70, go north on Kansas 177. This road was recently widened, creating new road cuts that allow you to see what lies beneath these gentle hills. You will notice layers of hard limestone alternating with layers of soft shale in shades of red and green. Both are the heritage of the Pennsylvanian Period of geologic history, 300 million years ago, when Kansas was covered by a shallow, oscillating sea. As the water changed depths, it left behind layers of shale in the shallow parts and limestone in the deeper parts.

Then, about 250 million years ago, during the Permian Period, the sea deposited flint (technically, it's chert, but has always been called flint locally) along with the limestone. Flint is silicon dioxide, the same chemical formula as glass, and it is harder than steel. During the past 60 million years, while water and wind have been eroding the rest of Kansas, the Flint Hills have resisted erosion because of this cap of hard rock.

The limestone/flint layer has saved the Flint Hills in another sense, too, because white settlers quickly learned that the shallow, rocky soils were not suited for farming. While much of the tallgrass prairie was plowed for farming, the Flint Hills were preserved and

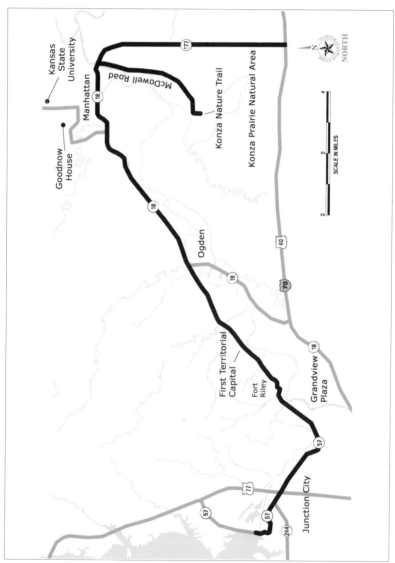

Tour 10: Manhattan to Junction City.

now contain the largest tract of tallgrass prairie in the world.

Just before you get to the bridge into Manhattan, turn left onto Riley County 901S, McDowell Creek Road. The road runs between the Kaw River and the hills, and it feels almost as though you are in two different places at once. On your right is the broad, flat floodplain where you will see white frame farmhouses surrounded by lush fields of corn and wheat, a typical Eastern farm scene. On your left, you will see stone ranch houses, stone barns, and stone fences tucked into the hills, cattle grazing around them, the image of the West. The contrast is perhaps most striking in winter, when the bottomland fields of winter wheat are brilliant green, and the tallgrass prairie is golden.

When you reach the sign for the Konza Prairie, turn in, and park at the trailhead. Konza Prairie Research Natural Area is 8,600 acres of virgin tallgrass prairie, which means it has never been plowed. It was once part of the 10,000-acre Dewey Ranch, purchased in 1872 by C.P. Dewey, a Chicago land speculator. C.P. Dewey and his son, Chauncy, kept adding to their empire in this area, particularly after a savage blizzard in 1886 forced many cattle ranchers to sell their land cheap. By 1926, the Deweys owned 30 large parcels of Flint Hills land. But their cattle enterprises, like those of so many whose land they had bought, eventually failed, and the mortgage holder repossessed the Dewey Ranch in 1930.

Two years later, George Davis purchased it, bringing his acreage in Kansas up to 70,000 and making him the largest landowner in the state. Davis also owned the Z Bar Ranch, which included the 10,984-acre parcel near Strong City that is now the Tallgrass Prairie National Preserve. He owned an even larger parcel in southwest Kansas that media magnate Ted Turner purchased in 1999.

The Nature Conservancy acquired the Konza in 1977 and turned it over to Kansas State University for management. For many years, the Konza was off limits to everyone but the scientists who conduct research here, but today a public trail will take you through stream and prairie habitats.

The self-guided nature trail loop is 2.8 miles. Pick up a brochure at the trailhead that will introduce you to the grasses and other plants that make up the tallgrass prairie and gallery forests along the streams. Go quietly, and you may see wildlife in the first "edge" area of the trail, where a cultivated field meets the riparian area along the stream. Turkeys and deer are common visitors here.

The first part of the hike has a steep hill that may be taxing,

Kings Creek runs through the Konza Prairie Research Natural Area in Riley County.

but it is well worth the effort. When you reach the ridge, you will look out on a nearly pristine landscape that stretches as far as the eye can see.

As you get accustomed to this splendor, you will begin to notice slight differences in the hills before you. Some are covered entirely in grass, some have trees stretching farther up the hillsides, some seem to have a different hue of green or gold. What you are observing are the results of many years of research to determine how fire and grazing affect prairie ecosystems.

The Konza is divided into watersheds, the portions of land where water runs off to a particular stream, ranging in size from 10 acres to 400 acres. Each watershed is treated differently, burned at different intervals or at different times of the year. Some are grazed by bison, which once roamed these hills by the millions before they were slaughtered to near extinction in the mid-1800s. In the future, some sections will be grazed by elk, another native grazer that no longer is found in Kansas.

At the radio tower, the self-guided nature trail heads downhill to the stream. If you want to see more, you can do the Kings Creek Loop, which is 4.7 miles, or go farther still on the Godwin Hill Loop, 6.1 miles. Maps for the longer loops are available near the radio tower.

As you walk, you may see some interesting wildlife if you follow the PEQ rule: Be patient, early, and quiet. Late is good, too, as many animals are more active at both sunrise and sunset. In midday, you may spot some of the more unusual animals living here—such as lizards basking in the sun on rocky outcrops.

The Great Plains skink is a small, slick, shiny lizard that sheds its tail easily when touched. The tail contains enough energy reserves to keep it twitching for several minutes, enough to distract a predator and allow the rest of the skink to escape. The tail will regrow within a few weeks, and can be shed again when needed.

Then there's the collared lizard, described by one biologist as having "a fearsome aspect that matches its malevolent personality." Males are bright green at the beginning of the breeding season, and they defend their territory by performing head bobs and push-ups to scare off intruders, including humans. Texas horned lizards are also occasionally seen. These spiny lizards look like little dinosaurs.

If you see a snake in the grassland, don't panic, as it is almost certainly harmless. Of the 13 species of snake found on Konza, only one—the copperhead—is venomous. This is the western edge of the copperhead's range, so they are not common, but they occasionally have been seen in rocky areas in oak woodlands, near streams or ponds.

Prairie plants

Among the plants, big bluestem is the star. This spectacular grass, which can reach 10 feet in a good year, is found in all but a few states in the continental United States, and in fact originated in the East, in the inland valleys of the Appalachians. But it is here in the Flint Hills that it finds the best conditions and flourishes. Big bluestem, sometimes called turkey foot for the shape of its flower head, crowds out most other plants on Konza, but scattered microsites favor other important grass species including little bluestem, Indian grass, and switchgrass.

Western wheatgrass can be found in small patches on clay soil, and eastern gammagrass is found in wet lowlands. Prairie cordgrass lives in very wet areas, around springs. And grama grass, more common in the shortgrass prairie of the West, can be found in some dry sites.

Despite the preponderance of grasses in terms of plant numbers, more than 80 percent of the species found in the Konza are

Fire on the prairie

The role of fire in the prairie has been particularly well explored here at Konza. Scientists now know that the major plants and animals on the prairie are most successful when the area burns every two to four years. This finding corresponds to historical records of the frequency of prairie fires before white settlement, when lightning sparked fires that went unimpeded by humans. If fires occur more frequently than every two years, the prairie is not as lush. If more than five years pass between fires, the plants suffer because they are choked by the litter of previous years' growth. Also, too few fires allow woody shrubs and trees to get established.

Research also has shown that the best time for a prairie fire, from the plants' perspective, is in late spring when the soil is moist. Fires burn up the litter of dead plants, and the layer of black ash warms the soil quickly. Fires also free some nutrients that were tied up in the plant litter, providing a shot of fertility to the deep-rooted grasses.

Fire also bares the soil so it can soak up rainfall, instead of having rain trapped on the dead plants above and evapo-

non-grasses. They are found in relatively small numbers, but they make up in color what they lack in quantity. Sixty-five species in the aster family—including the widespread heath asters and several kinds of sunflower—are found here. Gayfeather, blue false indigo, penstemons, wild roses, butterfly milkweed, yarrow, and goldenrod are just a few of the flowers that brighten the prairie from spring until fall.

If you've fallen in love with Konza Prairie by now, you will want to return for the biennial Fall Visitors Day, held in even-numbered years, when scientists lead tours of areas that are normally off limits to the public. Call 785-587-0441 for the date.

Manhattan

Head back into Manhattan, a lovely town of limestone build-

rating. All in all, a spring prairie fire gives the native grasses a strong start, and the blackened land starts to turn green within days after the fire.

Burning at other times of year can affect the prairie, too. Winter burns promote the success of non-grass plants like wildflowers, and burning in early to mid-spring promotes the growth of little bluestem, which is shorter and has a more orange color in fall and winter than big bluestem.

Not burning enables succession of woody species, and within a few decades, trees replace the grasses. As you look over the hills, see if you can identify burning regimens by the appearance of the prairie.

The success of the springtime burns here at Konza has convinced many ranchers that their land should be burned every couple of years, too, so the Flint Hills are full of smoke in spring. A prairie burn is an awesome sight, especially at night when the line of orange flames stretches against the black sky. But fires can be dangerous to those who don't know the plan; keep your distance, and, if smoke crosses the road, pull off until visibility improves.

Wildflowers, including the prairie coneflower, add contrasting colors to the green grasses at the Konza Prairie.

ings and tree-lined streets. There are two areas to find a bite to eat: downtown, including the enclosed mall there, and Aggieville, a small shopping area adjacent to the Kansas State University campus.

Goodnow House is a state historic site in the 1861 limestone house of Isaac Goodnow, one of the abolitionist founders of Manhattan. Nearby is the Riley County Historical Museum, with exhibits about local history from pioneer days to present.

Fort Riley

Take Kansas 18 southwest to Fort Riley, the state's largest military installation. It is also the second largest employer in the state, with 23,000 workers, and the tenth largest city, with 10,000 soldiers and 16,000 military family members stationed here. Fort Riley has been a training center for soldiers in every war of the 20th century, and untold numbers of Americans from all over the country have spent at least a few weeks here.

Fort Riley has 101,000 acres in which to train soldiers in every weapon system available in a heavy division. That explains the muffled booms you may have been hearing since you got into the Manhattan area. The 1st, 9th, and 10th Infantry Divisions train here. The fort also has the Army's largest railhead facility, which can load a division-sized unit in about five days.

First Territorial Capitol

As you drive down the wide main boulevard, Huebner Road, watch on your left for the old stone building known as the First Territorial Capitol. Even with the frequent shifting of the capital in the early days of Kansas, this building holds the record for the shortest time in service.

This site was chosen by the first territorial governor, Andrew Reeder, who established a free-state town called Pawnee here. Many settlers believed he convened the legislature in Pawnee for his own profit. All of the legislators who came were proslavery men elected in the bitterly contested March election in which Missourians crossed the state line and voted fraudulently. (See Chapter 6.)

Back in the free state towns of Lawrence and Manhattan, this legislature was known as the Bogus Legislature, and the laws it passed were called the Bogus Laws. The most despised law was one that made speaking against slavery a crime punishable by death. The 39 members of the first territorial legislature arrived on June 30, 1855, and voted on July 4 to move the capital to the Shawnee Methodist Mission in present-day Johnson County.

Four months after the brief legislative session, the War Department ordered a survey of Fort Riley's boundaries, and the town of Pawnee was found to be on military property. Army troops arrived, moved residents out of their homes, and razed all the buildings except the capitol, which became an army storehouse. The building fell into disrepair until 1907, when the Union Pacific Railroad undertook a complete restoration and in 1928 deeded it to the state. At this writing, it is operated as a museum by the Kansas State Historical Society, but budget cuts have made its future uncertain.

Kaw River Nature Trail

Just behind the First Territorial Capitol is a 1.75-mile hiking trail that will put you in the riparian area you've read so much about in this book. Take a stroll down the trail to the river bank (but don't get too close, because it has been known to collapse) where you will see the river, still showing debris from the flood of 1993. After you reach the bank, the path winds through the woods

An evolving outpost

Fort Riley is situated at the confluence of the Republican River and the Kansas River. John C. Fremont's 1843 expedition camped here and reported that it would be a good site for a town. Fremont also noted great numbers of elk, antelope, and Indians, who were gone not long after his first visit. In 1852, the Army chose the spot for a western outpost to protect travelers and traders on the Oregon and Santa Fe trails against raids by Indians.

In 1855, as the Army brought in laborers from Missouri to build the post, a cholera epidemic struck, and 70 people died. Nearly all were civilians, as the main body of troops was away on an Indian campaign. One of the most famous victims was Susan Fox, a young woman who was preparing for her wedding when cholera killed her. Her fiance found her body and buried her in her wedding dress near the railway bridge to the trolley station. Afterwards, residents of her home described strange noises and shrieks. A maid who was ironing by a window was so frightened when she thought she saw Susan staring in the window at her that she threw the iron through the glass. The post commander, irritated about the wild rumors of a ghost, paid a priest to perform an exorcism. Then, for good measure, he ordered the house razed. But reports of Susan's ghost still occur from time to time.

along the river bank, and marked posts identify various plants and other features typical of this type of habitat. Take time to appreciate the huge cottonwood trees towering overhead.

Main post

Farther along Huebner Road you will encounter the limestone buildings of the main post. Two good museums recount military history: The U.S. Cavalry Museum, housed in the 1855 hospital, explores the history of mounted soldiers, and the 1st Infantry Division Museum explains the history of the division known

After the Civil War, construction of the Kansas Pacific Railroad caused serious Indian uprisings, as the native tribes saw their chief source of food and income, the bison, being decimated. The Army decided it needed troops here to protect the railroad workers and settlers, and the 7th Cavalry was organized in 1866, with Lt. George A. Custer as second in command.

In 1892, a cavalry school was established, and it came to be known as one of the best in the world, producing extremely skilled mounted soldiers. Horse shows, hunts, and polo matches were a natural consequence of the horse emphasis. The Cavalry School Hunt, a colorful spectacle on Sunday mornings, caused the perception that life here was somewhat rarified and recreational and gave rise to the envious expression "the life of Riley."

Fort Riley was host to much disagreement over the role of the horse as the 20th century marched on, and horsemanship remained an important part of life here until World War II brought about its decline. The Cavalry School was discontinued in 1946, and, the following March, the last tactical horse unit was inactivated. Chief, the last horse in the cavalry, is buried at the fort, and a statue based on a Frederick Remington sketch is on his grave.

as "The Big Red One" from World War I to Desert Storm. You can also visit St. Mary's Chapel, the first stone church in Kansas, and the Main Post Chapel. Custer House, the only remaining set of officers quarters from the 1850s, is open for tours, and it offers period furnishings and displays representing the life of a 19th-century Army family. Despite its name, Lt. George Custer did not live here, but in another officers quarters that was destroyed by fire.

Bison

You might also stop at the Buffalo Corral; sometimes the bison come right up to the front of the pen, which is about as close as you could ever hope to get to a live bison. If they're in the back of the pen, you won't be able to see much. Most of the bison that once lived here are now roaming the Konza Prairie. A few years ago, a rare white calf was born here, which excited much interest among Native Americans because of a legend in which the Great Spirit takes the form of a white bison calf. Sadly, the calf died a few months after birth.

The bison, widely known as buffalo, was the center of life for Plains Indians before white contact. The buffalo hunt was an important season, as it provided the people with food, shelter, clothing, tools, and even toys for the children. Bison roamed the Plains and the mountain regions from Canada to Mexico in such huge numbers that early explorers were dumbfounded.

"The country was one black robe," said one writer.

"The plains were black and appeared as if in motion," wrote another.

The most commonly used estimate of their numbers is 60 million. Bison hunting by whites began with the fur trade in the 1600s, and by the early 1800s, 200,000 bison were killed annually for their robes. By the 1850s, there were many in government who advocated extermination of the buffalo as a way of exterminating the Indians who depended on them. Millions were slaughtered for their hides, which were shipped East, and by 1874, the last commercial hunt occurred. By 1893, an estimated 300 bison remained.

In 1905, President Theodore Roosevelt persuaded Congress to establish wildlife preserves to save the bison, and a 1929 inventory showed their numbers had slowly climbed to 3,385. By then, ranchers began to recognize the economic potential of bison, and breeding efforts increased.

Today, an estimated 150,000 bison are being raised in the United States for meat, which is touted as being nutrient-dense because of the proportion of protein, fat, minerals, and fatty acids compared to calories. About 20,000 are estimated to be living in Kansas, and Ted Turner's new ranch will add an additional 5,000 to the state total.

These producers are careful to call them by their correct scientific name, bison, now that water buffalo products are finding their way into the U.S. market. Bison are members of the *Bovidae* genus, same as cattle. Some ranchers are even treating the bison like cattle, sending them to a feedlot—the only bison feedlot in the United States is in Scott City, Kansas—to bring them to market weight. Kansas has some organic bison producers who let the animals live their entire lives in the wild and slaughter them in the pasture.

Bison command a good market price, but they are just a drop in the bucket of U.S. meat consumption. About 20,000 bison are slaughtered per year; 135,000 cattle are slaughtered every day.

Junction City

As you exit Fort Riley, you will cross a small bridge where the Republican and Smoky Hill rivers come together to form the Kaw. The junction of these two rivers is what gave the city its name. In the center of town, you will find many beautiful buildings of magnesium limestone quarried from the bluffs around the city.

This area was the site of a large Kansa Indian village before white settlement. The official Kansa reserve was nearby until its residents were removed to Council Grove in 1847. Exhibits pertaining to the Native American residents of the river junction can be found at the Geary County Historical Museum at 6th and

Adams, a limestone building that was previously the Junction City high school.

Milford Lake

If you still have time, swing by Milford Lake, the final Corps of Engineers reservoir in the Kansas River basin. Milford is the largest lake in the state, covering 15,000 acres in its multipurpose pool, more than twice that in its flood-control pool. Besides the usual lake attractions, Milford has a fish hatchery that you can visit, a nature center, and a new hiking trail along the Republican River.

For more information

- Konza Prairie, 785-587-0441; www.ksu.edu/biology/bio/major/konza.html.
- Manhattan Convention and Visitors Bureau, 501 Poyntz, Manhattan, KS 66502; www.manhattan.org.
- Goodnow House, 2309 Claflin Road, Manhattan, KS 66502; 785-565-6490; www.kshs.org/places/goodnow.htm.
- First Territorial Capitol, P.O. Box 2122, Fort Riley, KS 66442; 785-784-5535; www.kshs.org/places/firstter.htm.
- Fort Riley Museums, Fort Riley, KS 66442; 785-239-2737; www.riley.army.mil/.
- Geary County Convention and Visitors Bureau, P.O. Box 1846, Junction City, KS 66441; 800-528-2489; www.junctioncity.org/cvb/.

Selected Bibliography

Ambrose, Stephen E. 1996. *Undaunted Courage: Meriwether Lewis, Thomas Jefferson, and the Opening of the American West.* New York: Touchstone.

Buchanan, Rex, and James R. McCauley. 1987. *Roadside Kansas: A Traveler's Guide to Its Geology and Landmarks.* Lawrence: University Press of Kansas.

Collins, Joseph T., ed. 1985. *Natural Kansas.* Lawrence: University Press of Kansas.

Dary, David. 1984. *True Tales of Old-Time Kansas.* Lawrence: University Press of Kansas.

Dary, David. 1987. *More True Tales of Old-Time Kansas.* Lawrence: University Press of Kansas.

Fitzgerald, Daniel. 1988. *Ghost Towns of Kansas: A Traveler's Guide.* Lawrence: University Press of Kansas.

Franzwa, Gregory M. 1997. *The Oregon Trail Revisited.* Tucson: The Patrice Press.

Gress, Bob, and George Potts. 1993. *Watching Kansas Wildlife: A Guide to 101 Sites.* Lawrence: University Press of Kansas.

Hann, David. 1999. *Kansas Past: Pieces of the 34th Star.* Lawrence, Kansas: Penthe Publishing.

Hauber, Catherine M. 1999. *Hiking Guide to Kansas.* Lawrence: University Press of Kansas.

Laird, Betty, and Martha Parker. 1976. *Soil of Our Souls: Histories of the Clinton Lake Area Communities.* Overbrook, Kansas: Parker-Laird Enterprises.

Reichman, O.J. 1987. *Konza Prairie: A Tallgrass Natural History.* Lawrence: University Press of Kansas.

Richmond, Robert W. 1992. *Kansas: A Pictorial History.* Lawrence: University Press of Kansas.

Rowe, Elfriede Fischer. 1981. *More About Wonderful Old Lawrence.* Lawrence, Kansas: House of Usher.

Shortridge, James R. 1977 and 1988. *Kaw Valley Landscapes: A Traveler's Guide to Northeastern Kansas.* Lawrence: University Press of Kansas.

Socolofsky, Homer E., and Huber Self. 1988. *Historical Atlas of Kansas.* Tulsa: University of Oklahoma Press.

Stephens, H.A. 1969. *Trees, Shrubs and Woody Vines in Kansas.* Lawrence: Regents Press of Kansas.

Stokes, Donald and Lillian. 1991. *The Bluebird Book: The Complete Guide to Attracting Bluebirds.* New York: Little, Brown & Co.

The WPA Guide to 1930s Kansas. 1984. Lawrence: University Press of Kansas.

Index